THE REAL
ARTHUR
MILLER

THE REAL
ARTHUR
MILLER

THE PLAYWRIGHT WHO CARED

ANDREW NORMAN

WHITE OWL

AN IMPRINT OF PEN & SWORD BOOKS LTD
YORKSHIRE ~ PHILADELPHIA

First published in Great Britain in 2024 by
PEN AND SWORD WHITE OWL
An imprint of
Pen & Sword Books Ltd
Yorkshire – Philadelphia

ISBN 978 1 39904 073 0

Typeset in Times New Roman 12/16 by
SJmagic DESIGN SERVICES, India.
Printed and bound in the UK by CPI Group (UK) Ltd, Croydon, CR0 4YY.

Pen & Sword Books Limited incorporates the imprints of Atlas, Archaeology,
Aviation, Discovery, Family History, Fiction, History, Maritime, Military,
Military Classics, Politics, Select, Transport, True Crime, Air World,
Frontline Publishing, Leo Cooper, Remember When, Seaforth Publishing,
The Praetorian Press, Wharncliffe Local History, Wharncliffe Transport,
Wharncliffe True Crime, White Owl and After the Battle.

For a complete list of Pen & Sword titles please contact

PEN & SWORD BOOKS LIMITED
George House, Units 12 & 13, Beevor Street, Off Pontefract Road,
Barnsley, South Yorkshire, S71 1HN, England
E-mail: enquiries@pen-and-sword.co.uk
Website: www.pen-and-sword.co.uk

or
PEN AND SWORD BOOKS
1950 Lawrence Rd, Havertown, PA 19083, USA
E-mail: uspen-and-sword@casematepublishers.com
Website: www.penandswordbooks.com

Contents

Acknowledgements

Jean Bennett; Bernard Burgess; Paul G. Kengor; Jessica Sutcliffe.

Bentley Historical Library, Ann Arbor, Michigan, USA.

I am deeply grateful to my beloved wife Rachel, for all her help and support.

Foreword

During his lifetime Arthur Miller was affronted in numerous ways, either personally, or vicariously through the experiences of others. For example:

By the way his immigrant family had come to financial grief in the Great Depression – the financial and industrial slump of 1929 and subsequent years – when it's family members had worked so hard to establish themselves in their adopted country, the USA. And this, through no fault of their own.

By the anti-Semitism that existed in the USA and elsewhere in the 1930s, culminating in the Nazi Holocaust in which so many people of his own ethnic group, the Jews, together with millions of other innocents, perished.

By the way he and others, including many connected with the arts, were persecuted for alleged communist sympathies in the McCarthy 'witch-hunts' of the late 1940s and 1950s in the USA.

By the way that atheism, to which he himself subscribed, was considered to be subversive and unpatriotic.

By the way religion is hijacked for political purposes.

By the way that the 'American Dream' was generally portrayed as something to which everybody could aspire: a concept by the standards of which, most people were failures and considered themselves to be so, to their own detriment. In other words, by embracing the concept of the American Dream, they were generally setting themselves up to fail.

By the aggressive warmongering of politicians who engaged in unnecessary, pointless and costly conflicts, notably the Vietnam War (1 November 1955 to 30 April 1975).

Also, Miller bewailed the fact that his plays, in which many of these themes were reflected, were for many years not appreciated in his own country. Whereas in Europe, and even in China and Russia, they were recognised for being the masterpieces that they undoubtedly are, for obvious reasons!

While others might have buckled under the strain of inhabiting a world with which they felt so much at odds, Miller soldiered relentlessly on. He refused to be silenced, was determined that his message be heard and meanwhile, was swift to applaud the occasional acts of kindness and self-sacrifice that he encountered along the way.

Finally, he strove to illuminate a path to a better way and in doing so, offered hope to the inhabitants of the flawed and troubled world in which he found himself, not just in the USA but also elsewhere.

Chapter 1

The Miller Family: from Austro-Hungary to New York City

In his autobiography *Timebends* (published on 1 November 1987 when he was aged 72), Miller stated that his father, Isidore (born 15 September 1884, given name Isadore Müeller) 'had arrived in New York all alone from the middle of Poland before his seventh birthday', his family having already relocated to the USA.[1]

Isidore's parents, Samuel (b. 1858, given name Shmnel Müeller) and Dora (b. 1866, née Keil), who were Jewish, had originated from the small town of Radomyśl Wiekl in Galicia, now Poland but then, part of the Austro-Hungarian Empire.[2] They were married in August 1881.

Some time prior to 1894, Miller's paternal grandparents, Samuel and Dora emigrated with their three sons and three daughters to the USA. The sons were Abraham ('Abe', b. c.1882); Mordecai ('Max', b. 1887); William (b. 1890). The daughters were Annie (b. 1881); Augusta ('Gussie', b. 1888); and Sadie ('Sarah, b. 1891). However, another son, Isidore (b. 15 September 1884, Miller's father-to-be), was left behind, and Miller believed that he had been left in an 'institution'. However, in the year 1894, Isidore, now aged 10, finally arrived at Castle Garden, Manhattan, to be met by his older brother Abraham. Isidore was taken to the family home, a tenement on Stanton Street, Borough of Manhattan, New York City. By now, every member of the family was engaged in sewing for the manufacture of clothing. This even applied to the children, when they were not at school.[3] Here, 'in two rooms the eight of them lived and worked, sewing the great, long, many-buttoned cloaks that were the fashion then'. The business rapidly expanded, and more employees were taken on.

Isidore, said Miller, 'used to say that he would always be [i.e. had been] sleeping with idiots, and I have a feeling that he may have been in some kind of institution'.

Said Miller of his father, 'they sent him to school for about six months, figuring he had enough' by then. 'He never learned how to spell; he never learned how to figure. Then he went right back into the shop.' By the time Isidore was 12, he 'was employing two other boys to sew sleeves on coats, alongside him in some basement workshop.[4] They were cutting out coats, ladies' coats. And he had two employees who were 10 years old'. His father told him just before he died, said Miller with a chuckle:

> he did not regard that as unusual. I think he felt that he was well along in years to be starting. I think that they were still in a time of civilisation where people died at 42 or 45; a lot of them did, of various diseases. So that you got on your way at 16 and you were where you wanna be by 22 or 23: you were a middle-aged man at 30, 33, or 34, and you were dead when you were 45.

When Isidore was aged 14, his father sent him 'on the road with a trunk of coats he was supposed to sell to various stores along the railroad lines'.[5] The following year he was employed by Miller & Sons – now the name of the family firm – as a salesman, selling woollen coats in the great cities of Cleveland, Ohio; Chicago, Illinois; and Minneapolis, Minnesota.

On 31 December 1911, at the age of 27, Isidore married Augusta (b. 18 March 1891, New York City), given name 'Gittel', née Barnett).[6]

Augusta was the daughter of Louis, a clothing manufacturer, and his wife Rose (née Leibel), who were both Jewish. Her parents originated from the same small town of Radomyśl Wiekl in Galicia as Isidore's parents had originated from. The Gittels had left Poland for the USA in the late 1870s and subsequently moved to New York City. It was only after they married, that Augusta discovered that her husband Isidore was illiterate.[7]

Frances ('Fran', née Resnick), wife of Miller's elder brother Kermit, said of Isidore and Augusta, 'It was an arranged marriage. But for a woman of her ability to be married off to a man who couldn't read or write!' By contrast, Augusta was literary and well read, and she was also musical. Of his mother, Augusta ('Gussie'), Miller said: 'You know, she could read a novel in an afternoon. She was the fastest reader I have ever met in my life. Not only that, but she'd remember it for the rest of her life.'[8]

According to Frances, 'I think Gussie taught [Isidore] how to read and sign his name', and Miller believed Augusta 'knew she was being wasted, but she respected him a lot and that made up for it, until he really crashed economically, and she got angry with him'.[9]

Isidore and Augusta's first child, Kermit Miller, was born on 5 October 1912. He was followed by Arthur Asher Miller, born on 17 October 1915 at West 111th Street, Harlem, a Borough of Manhattan. Shortly afterwards, the family moved to 45, 110th Street, Harlem to a luxury apartment.[10] This reflected their increasing affluence. On 1 June 1922 their third child, Joan Maxine Miller was born.

After the First World War, Isidore left the family business and in 1921, at the age of 37, he created the Miltex Coat & Suit Company, in which enterprise he was joined by his brothers. The company grew and eventually became one of the largest manufacturers in the country, with approximately 1,000 employees.[11] Isidore, said Miller, 'ended up being the support of the entire family'.

Having become wealthy, Miller said:

We lived in Manhattan then, on 110th Street facing the park. It was a beautiful apartment on the sixth floor. We had a chauffeur-driven car. The family was well fixed. It was the '20s and I remember our mother and father going to a show every weekend and coming back Sunday morning. She would be playing the sheet music of the musicals and we would fight about who was going to sing with her and who wasn't going to sing. [Pointing at Kermit] … Generally he wasn't going to sing![12]

For his own part, Miller believed that his creative talent came from his mother. 'The world, essentially, is not what we call real, and these arts [i.e. literature, painting, and music] are attempting to approach that world' he said, as if life to him was akin to a dream. 'And it all comes from my mother. You know, its always coming from somewhere. She was that way. She idolised writers, artists, pianists and so on.'

According to Kermit, Augusta 'could sing, she could play the piano, she could draw, she was a hell of a bridge player', and Miller added: 'She used to dance on the table on New Year's Eve. As for the Miller family's diet, they ate kosher food 'except when she started making bacon. She loved bacon.'[13]

When the Great Depression came, said Miller, the people of the USA regarded it as 'their fault. They would rather take the blame themselves than blame the system.' Previously, 'one's money had come out of the air'; the money was 'just there. You just picked it off the stock market, painlessly. Now, suddenly, money was pain. To get it [i.e. the act of striving to acquire it] was painful.'[14] This was because jobs were scarce or non-existent and wages were low.

Two of Miller's maternal uncles, who were both salesmen, moved to Brooklyn in the 1920s from Upper New York State. One was

Lee Balsam, who married Augusta's sister, Esther. The other was Manny Newman, who married another sister, Anna. Newman was one day to inspire Miller to write a play, *Death of a Salesman*, in which Newman would reappear as the iconic character 'Willy Loman'.

Chapter 2

Childhood and Youth

In 1980, on British television arts magazine show The South Bank Show, Miller spoke about his childhood to British broadcaster, author and parliamentarian, Melvin Bragg. Bragg, for his part, described Miller as 'a wonderfully open person to interview. He is a joy to talk to and he is fantastically honest.'

Said Miller, 'I had nobody in my family who was remotely connected with even reading a book much. My mother read, but the rest of them didn't.' However, there was 'a powerful pressure' applied to those newly arrived immigrants to acquire learning and 'that's what you did'. Therefore, he said with a chuckle, 'becoming an artist' was not something 'as outlandish as it should seem. I think that there was, more than I was aware of, an expectation that doing something in the arts was not incredible.' In the 1920s, the family:

> was the unit of the world, much more than probably would ever be again, in any Western society. Probably, I'd connect it with immigration, and with living in a society that you couldn't expect much of. One's strength came solely from the family and one had 'to achieve everything by oneself.

Miller described just how hostile the outside world was in the USA of the 1920s: 'You were safe at home, but you weren't safe once you got out of the house. The world was fundamentally an arena in which you threw yourself and wrestled with the lions.'

In Harlem, said Miller, there were Jews, Italians, Irish, Blacks, Puerto Ricans, 'so it was on the edge of a slum'. It was a neighbourhood where 'people were constantly fighting and stealing'. When Miller saw his first Charlie Chaplin films, he failed to understand the humour because Chaplin: 'was stealing all the time, and it was just like real life. You couldn't leave a bicycle around anywhere. You couldn't leave a baseball glove, or a skate, or whatever. You carried everything with you, like a pack animal.'[1]

Of the relationship between Miller and his mother Augusta, Kermit's wife Frances said, 'I think she tried to rule and divide the kids.' When asked who was his mother's favourite, him or his brother Kermit, Miller answered:

> I think I was. For example, if I didn't want to go to school, I'd start limping around. My mother immediately caught on and she'd say, 'You don't want to have to go to school today, you're limping', and we'd both go to some place and have oysters. She saw mysterious things in the air from time to time. She had feelings from people. She once sat up in bed in the middle of the night and said, 'My mother died.' And indeed, at that moment her mother had died. It was spooky![2]

In fact, Augusta's mother Rose actually died on 10 February 1940.

When the great Wall Street Crash occurred in September 1929, Miller was aged 13. On 'Black Tuesday', the fourth and last day of the crash, 16 million shares were sold on Wall Street, the New York stock exchange, and the economy collapsed. The impact on the Miller family was severe and immediate: 'First, the chauffeur was let go; the summer bungalow was discarded; the last of her [Augusta's] jewellery had to be pawned or sold, and then another step down, the move to Brooklyn.' But, Miller said, their family was not alone. 'I used to pal around with half a dozen guys and all their fathers were simply blown out of the water.'

Miller described how his mother Augusta had mixed feelings towards her husband Isidore in regard to this financial catastrophe, 'I could not avoid awareness of my mother's anger at this waning of his powers; a certain sneering contempt for him, that filtered through her voice'. On the other hand, said Miller, when his father lost his money, his mother felt 'terrible pity' for him. As for Isidore himself:

> So much of his authority sprang from the fact that he was a very successful businessman, and he always knew what he was doing, and suddenly, nothing. He didn't know where he was. It was absolutely not his fault. It was the great crash of the [19] '29 '30 '31 period.[3]

In 1932 Miller, now aged 17, graduated from Brooklyn's Abraham Lincoln High School, but not with distinction! 'I got through high school', he said, but: 'I had such a miserable record that I couldn't get into a decent university, so I went to work on a full-time basis.' In fact, he commenced as a waiter in the Catskills Hotel. 'It was the most elegant hotel in the Catskills [a mountainous district of south-eastern New York State]', he said, but 'I was the worst waiter!'

In 1933, Miller was temporary employed by his father in his garment factory, a job which he disliked. As a result, he wrote a short story *In Memoriam* (published in *The New Yorker* on 17 December 1995). This was a precursor to his evocative and monumental play, *Death of a Salesman* (1949), about which more will be said shortly. Finally, in that same year of 1933, he said, 'I landed a hell of a job in an automobile parts warehouse.' But it was not a case of 'all work and no play'. He travelled 'an hour and a half on the subway every morning, and I started reading what they call "thick" books'. This experience ultimately resulted in the play, *A Memory of Two Mondays*, which opened at the Coronet Theatre on Broadway on 29 September 1955.

'I remember reading Dostoevsky once', said Miller, referring to the novel *The Brothers Karamazov*,[4] which is concerned with the concepts of God, free will and morality. 'I was staring in space for weeks, to think how a human being could write that! So, I saved up 500 dollars. In 1934, and 'after much pleading', the University of Michigan agreed to accept him to study journalism.

According to Miller, Kermit did not go to university; being the eldest son of Jewish family, for him the family must always come first. (In fact, Kermit did attend the University of New York, but only for one year.) Kermit accepted that responsibility, 'which he took very seriously. And so, as time went on, he became loaded with responsibility for the family business. I escaped, thank God!'[5]

Chapter 3

The University of Michigan (1934 to 1938): Early Success: Miller the Idealist

In autumn 1934, Miller entered the University of Michigan, situated at Ann Arbor, a city west of the city of Detroit – he had worked to save up the money to support himself there. Prior to this he had attended City College, New York City, for about three weeks in the evenings. The college was founded as the Free Academy of the City of New York in 1847 by wealthy businessman and President of the Board of Education, Townsend Harris. It would provide children of immigrants and the poor, access to free higher education based on academic merit alone.[1] One problem for Miller, however, was his inability to stay awake, on account of working during the daytime.

According to Miller, he chose the University of Michigan 'because at that time it was probably the only university in the United States that had an active interest in creative writing. It was also the fact that the tuition was so cheap, and money was difficult to come by.' Also, the University of Michigan 'was not an aristocratic institution, that meant a lot to me'. But then 'since they took me in, they couldn't have been very aristocratic!'.

Did Miller's family think it odd that he was leaving New York for the Midwest (northern central region of the USA)? 'For a young guy, it was a great adventure,' he said. 'I thought of it as the "Wild West".' However, he 'was amazed that in Detroit, they had the same cars we had in New York', which was 618 miles away.

While at the University of Michigan, Miller worked as a reporter and night editor for the student newspaper, *Michigan Daily*, which reported both local and national news. When he started to win prizes for his plays, Miller ceased writing for the *Daily* in order to concentrate on this aspect of his life. He also lost his 'impulse to do journalism' because, Cassie admitted creating a good story is more important to him than the facts! 'So, I found I wasn't really made to be a reporter.' However, unlike with journalism, where he had been on the payroll, this: 'wasn't the case in the theatre. You were completely on your own there and you could easily starve to death. But I decided to pursue the theatre because I loved it.'

Was Miller able to visit home during his time at the university? 'Well, I got back during the Christmas vacation and that was about it. I usually had to work during the spring vacation. So, I got back once each year.'

As regards his tutors, said Miller, 'I had a wonderful teacher named Erich Walter, who later became Dean of the University. And Professor Walter directed me towards Kenneth Rowe.' Erich A. Walter (1897–1977) was Associate Professor of English, who subsequently became Dean of Students. Kenneth Thorpe Rowe (1900–1988) was Professor of Playwriting and Drama.

It was as a student in Eric Walter's class, 'that I wrote my first play', said Miller. This was in spring 1936, and the play was entitled, *No Villain*. When asked why he had written a play, rather than a story or a novel, he replied: 'I've never been sure, but it was like the difference for an artist between a sculpture and a drawing. It seemed more tangible.'

On the subject of playwriting, he declared: 'The theatre has a higher mission. It has had, for two or three thousand years, a civilising impact on man. And it remains yet the tribune [i.e. forum], where citizens such as myself may address, quite simply, plainly, and over empty air, his fellow citizen.'

In a wider context, Miller was part of a revolution. Soldiers returning from the First World War had made a tremendous sacrifice, and they were mindful that many of their comrades had made the ultimate sacrifice. 'Now it's our turn,' was the attitude, and this chimed perfectly with the aspirations of creative artists such as Miller, whose plays had ordinary people as their heroes and heroines. This was in contrast to the previous century, where plays, poems and novels were largely composed by, and accessible to, only the upper classes of society. As for *No Villain*, Miller continued: 'Working day and night, with a few hours of exhausted sleep sprinkled through the week, I finished the play in five days. It was about an industrial conflict and a father and his two sons: the most autobiographical dramatic work I would ever write!'

Said Judi Herman, editor of *Jewish Renaissance* magazine:

> The plot is what would become familiar Miller territory. The family tensions between fathers and sons here, in a New York Jewish family, all bound up in a moral dilemma that explores the contradictions between soulless capitalism and the hopes and desires of the individual. Would-be communist 'Arny', comes home from university to find his father's coat business on the point of collapse, precipitated by a recently unionised workers' strike that stops him shipping his output to customers. His struggling father, 'Abe' and older brother, 'Ben' urge Arny to help them save the business by getting out the orders, but Arny is trapped between loyalty to both his own family and a wider cause.[2] [I.e. Arny's desire to become a writer.]

No Villain was clearly autobiographical, with Miller vicariously reliving the desperate struggles of his own family during the Great Depression.

'Subsequently', Miller continued, 'I went to Professor Rowe,' to whom he became greatly indebted. Rowe, he declared:

> taught me really only one thing, and that was that I could hold the stage with dialogue. And he acquainted me with the history of the theatre and with the development of various forms: it was a quick way of getting educated. I was gunning for a Hopwood Award, which at the University of Michigan was the student equivalent of the Nobel [Prize].

The Avery Hopwood Award was a major scholarship founded by US playwright, J. Avery Hopwood (1882–1928) and awarded by the University of Michigan:

> But I had two jobs and a full academic schedule, and between dishwashing three times a day and feeding three floors of mice in a genetics laboratory in the woods at the edge of town, I would fall into bed each night exhausted.

Nonetheless, Miller duly won the Hopwood Award for *No Villain*. The citation read as follows:

Award in drama 1936

Prize $250

No Villain

A play by Arthur A. Miller

'I had won the Hopwood, 250 dollars for a week's work!, I wasn't really expecting to win anything … The idea of winning was really very remote. I decided to write a play, principally because at that time the theatre was the insurgent, left-wing, revolutionary theatre.'[3] Clearly, at this time of his life, Miller was a fired-up idealist who wanted to change the world!

It had taken Miller two years 'to save up the 500 dollars to come to Michigan', and he was now over the moon!. 'From the beginning writing meant freedom, the spreading of wings. I had never known such exhilaration. It was as though I had levitated and left the world below.' However, it was not until December 2015 that *No Villain* premiered at the Old Red Lion Theatre, London.[4]

In 1937, Miller won his second Avery Hopwood Award for *Honors at Dawn*. This is the story of 'Harry', who believes in the 'American Dream': the idea that anyone in the USA from whatever race, creed or social class can be successful, that 'upward mobility' is possible for all.

Harry goes to university. His brother, Max, is a mechanic at a car-parts factory. When the owner of the factory, who is a major donor to the university, 'insists that radicals should be dismissed from the university as the price of the company's support', Harry, who is 'prepared to compromise his values', becomes an informer; whereas Max, refuses.[5] Here, again, Miller is writing about the trials and tribulations of ordinary people in a cruel and unfair world.

It was also while at the University of Michigan that Miller met his wife-to-be, Mary Grace Slattery.

Miller would have loved to have debated matters with his father Isidore, with whom he never had an argument, and he lamented the fact that he was unable to do so. In his plays, he would often return to the problematic relationships between fathers and sons.

Miller the Idealist

Aside from his own and his family's personal experiences of life, and in particular of living through the Great Depression, Miller's outlook was shaped by the political and economic theories of German philosopher Karl Heinrich Marx (1818–1883), and social scientist Friedrich Engels (1820–1895). Their theories evolved to form the basis for the theory and practise of communism.[7] 'The first mention of Marxism I ever heard,' Miller said, 'was on a clear, full day in 1932.' (He was aged 17 at the time.[6]) 'This day's overturning of all I knew of the world' and revolutionised his ideas:

> For me, as for millions of young people then and since, the concept of a classless society had a disarming sweetness that called forth the generosity of youth. The *true* condition of man, it seemed, was the complete opposite of the competitive system I had assumed was normal, with all its mutual hatreds and conniving. [Whereas, with Marxism] Life could be a comradely embrace: people helping one another rather than looking for ways to trip each other up.[8]

Chapter 4

The Second World War (1 September 1939 to 2 September 1945): Marriage (1st) to Mary Grace Slattery (5 August 1940)

In the 1930s, 'anti-Semitism in the United States was rampant, it was open,' said Miller. 'For example, many people had to go to Europe to become doctors. They weren't admitted to [New York City's] Columbia University. Almost all of the American universities had a quota on Jews, and it was very small.' To add insult to injury, Miller continued, 'the largest radio audience in the United States was for a man who was quoting Goebbels all the time'. Joseph Goebbels was a Nazi politician and Reich Minister for Propaganda. As for the person who was quoting Goebbels, this was Canadian/US citizen, Father Charles E. Coughlin (1891–1979) from Detroit, Michigan: 'He had the largest audience excepting for FDR [Franklin Delano Roosevelt (1882–1945), Democrat and 32nd President of the USA from 1933 until his death in 1945]. He was saying how wonderfully the Nazis had dealt with unemployment; how fine it was that they were defending their racial purity. This was from a Catholic priest.'

> I remember walking down the street in Broadway one day, a hot day in the middle of July, and all the windows were open. I think it was a Sunday afternoon. And from

one house after another you could hear that voice, and it was sneering, raucous. He was a real rabble-rouser. He blamed the Jews for the Depression. That was the fundamental thing. The moneylenders had been thrown out of the temple, but they were back in. They controlled the currency; they controlled the big corporations; they controlled everything, secretly. They were the secret demon underlying the troubles of the state.

I was a worker in those days. I was out driving trucks and the rest of it, and you could cut it [anti-Semitism] with a knife. It was brutal, and it was open. There was no question about it. So, Jews were already positioned, vis-à-vis the society. They weren't being killed. They were simply being gently, but firmly, kept out of the mainstream. No big corporations had Jewish executives. It was unheard of.

When asked how Jewish *he* was, Miller replied, 'Absolutely Jewish, sure.' However, from his father Isidore, he said, he had 'inherited … the attitude of being an American more than a Jew'.[1]

Miller's thoughts can scarcely be imagined. Having immigrated to the USA in order to better themselves, members of his family had suffered all the hardships of the Depression and now, as Jews, were experiencing blatant and sustained racism on a daily basis. 'Therefore, you were driven to the left,' he said, 'because the right was not interested in these problems, nor were most liberals. It was too dangerous.'

In June 1939, the German ocean liner MS *St Louis*, captained by Gustav Schröder, brought 900 or so German-Jewish citizens from Germany to the coast of Miami, where it was anticipated that it would be allowed to dock in New York Harbour. This was in order that the passengers might be granted asylum in the USA. According to Miller:

it was not permitted to land. And then they went from here to Cuba where, from the studies I've read, the Americans did not want the Cuban government, which was then a dictatorship of the right, to let them in, because it would show up what we had done and reveal the cruelty of what we had done. Nobody was interested in confronting this thing, and they were sent back to Germany. I presume they were all killed.[2]

The Second World War commenced on 1 September 1939 when Adolf Hitler launched his invasion of Poland. On 5 August 1940, Miller married Mary Grace Slattery (b. 4 June 1915 in Lakewood, Ohio, to Matthew Thomas Slattery and his wife, Julia (née Siedel)). Mary was working as a stenographer at a medical publishing house, and the couple set up home at 18 Schermerhorn Street, Brooklyn. On 7 December 1941, the Japanese attacked the US fleet at Pearl Harbor, which led to the USA entering the Second World War on the side of the Allies.

The Millers' daughter, Jane (b. 7 September 1944), said of Mary: 'She worked in publishing. She was literary. I mean, she read everything. She was a rebel.' From what Jane said, Mary, like her husband Arthur, had rejected religion: 'She didn't like going to church. She stopped as soon as she could.' Mary's younger brother Robert ('Bob' or 'Bobby', b. 31 May 1947) agreed. His mother was: 'a Catholic woman, raised in the Midwest, who rebelled against all of that. They were all Republicans; she was a Democrat.' Mary 'moved to New York with a Jew (Miller)', continued Bob, 'and coming out of Michigan to New York was a dream come true.'

Of her father Jane said: 'You can see in the letters to Mary that he's quite puppyish with her, he really wants her approval, and he wants to please her.' Also, and not surprisingly, 'they went to the theatre all the time'. As for Miller, in a letter to Mary, he demonstrated his tender and caring nature towards his wife:

'Dear Sweet, I never quite realised how much I need you. Really, I sometimes ache with loneliness for you and I keep swearing over and over again, never to give you any unhappiness. Love, Art.'[3] Alas, this was all to change!

From November 1942 to April 1943, Miller was employed at the Brooklyn Navy Yard, a shipyard and industrial complex located in Brooklyn:

> I was rejected for the army because of a wounded leg that I had as a result of playing football, stupidly, in high school. I wanted to do something that was related to the war effort, so I took a job there. But at the same time, I was writing programs for radio. I'd do that in the daytime and work 11 hours at night in the yard. I was a ship fitter's helper, and I finally became a ship fitter. It was a terrific experience. It was wonderful work, although I never did understand how we managed to get ships out of the yard and onto the high seas without sinking, because few of us knew very much about anything. The yard before the war had 6,000 workers in it, who were highly trained people. During the war it had 60,000, and we were all loafers from every kind of position in society, and nobody knew a ship from a hole in the wall. How we managed to repair ships is an amazement to me, but they floated![4]

In 1943, Miller attended a course of study in Brooklyn on the subject of Marxism. On 7 September 1944, Mary gave birth to their daughter, Jane Ellen Miller.

What of his elder brother Kermit? Having been commissioned into the US Army in 1943, Kermit achieved the rank of captain and was sent to Europe with the 'Yankee Division' (US Army's 26th Infantry Division, based in Boston Massachusetts). As mentioned, despite being drafted, Miller was rejected by the US Army on account of a damaged knee. However, 'by that time I was on my way as a writer, writing scripts for radio,' he said.

Having landed on the Normandy beaches on 6 June 1944, Kermit subsequently:

> led his infantry patrol towards the Ardennes Forest on the German-Belgian border. During the Battle of the Bulge [16 December 1944 to 25 January 1945, the last major German offensive of the war], he was held down by enemy fire in a snowy foxhole. Despite frostbite on his feet, he carried a [wounded] fellow soldier on his back to safety and the field hospital. Before being properly healed, he asked to be returned to his squadron, and when the request was denied, he got himself out of bed, dressed, and returned to the front anyway. In sincere admiration [Arthur] Miller dedicated his book about soldiers, *Situation Normal* ... to Kermit.

Kermit was discharged in 1945 and awarded the Purple Heart, a US decoration for those wounded or killed in action (established in 1782 and re-established in 1932). However, he was now suffering from shell shock and battle fatigue. To make matters worse for Kermit, the cure was as bad as the illness. He: 'received a series of electric shock treatments as part of his rehabilitation treatment; these led to bouts of depression and forgetfulness for the rest of his life'.[5]

On 14 February 1945, in Stamford, Connecticut, Kermit married Frances Resnick, (b. 2 October 1917), a Jewish woman from Coney Island, New Jersey. Her parents were both from Ukraine: her mother Anna from Odessa, and her father Harry from Kyiv. This was Frances's second marriage. She would bear him a son, Ross.

The Second World War ended in Europe on 8 May 1945, and in the Far East on 2 September 1945 with the formal surrender of Japan.

29

Chapter 5

The Man Who Had All the Luck (1944): *All My Sons* (1947): *The Hook* (1947)

Arthur Miller's Broadway debut came on 23 November 1944, when *The Man Who Had All the Luck* premiered at the Forrest Theatre. 'The question behind the play is how much of our lives we make and how much are made by circumstance.' The play: 'was about a young man who lived in a small town in the Middle West. He can't seem to do anything wrong, and he gradually grows to fear that his fate is building up a thunder cloud which is going to strike him, and he becomes quite paranoid.'

Unfortunately, the play closed after only six performances. This was Miller's 'first introduction to show business', and the reviews of the play were poor.

After this setback, Miller was determined that he 'was not going to be attacked, or destroyed, or eaten alive' by the critics. Nevertheless, he said: 'I resolved that after the failure of *The Man Who Had All the Luck*, I was never going to write another play. I didn't want to be a 30-year-old would-be playwright. There are so many other things you can do with your life.' Instead, Miller proceeded to write a novel, entitled *Focus*, which, he said, 'was reasonably successful'.[1] In fact, *Focus*, published in November 1945, was to be Miller's only published novel. In it, he tackled the issue of anti-Semitism in the USA.

Their son Bob described just how supportive Mary was to her husband during this difficult period in their lives: 'she was the one who was paying the rent. And Dad sat down to write *Focus*, because he thought, "Maybe I'm not a playwright, maybe I've got to pay the rent somehow else".' Here, once again, Mary came to the rescue: 'She got the publisher she was working with to publish it [*Focus*], after he'd snapped it around [offered it] to some other places.' (Bob would go on to produce the film *Focus* in 2001 with businessman, politician, philanthropist, and author Michael R. Bloomberg)

Despite himself, Miller found the lure of playwriting and the theatre to be irresistible. 'And then I got sucked back into the theatre again,' he said, 'which was more of a natural medium for me anyway.[2] What I did was to decide that I would write a play one more time. This time, I took over two years to write it.'[3] The play was *All My Sons*.

All My Sons premiered at the Coronet Theatre on Broadway on 29 January 1947. He had already written 'about ten plays by that time', he said.[4] The theme of the play is how an overpowering love of money on the part of its protagonist 'Joe Keller' can create a lifetime of misery. Miller's mother-in-law, Julia, had unknowingly triggered the idea for the play, he said, when she had:

> gossiped, about a young girl somewhere in central Ohio who turned her father in to the FBI [Federal Bureau of Investigation: Domestic Intelligence and Security Service of the USA and its principal law enforcement agency] for having manufactured faulty aircraft parts during the war.
>
> This kind of placid American backyard was not ordinarily associated, at least in 1947, with murder and suicide. This was a son who was discovering the failing of a father and levelling a judgement upon him which is very harsh.

Years later, his daughter Rebecca (b. 1962, by his third wife, Ingeborg) asked Miller whether he had begun with a character when he had started to write *All My Sons*; 'Yes,' he replied: 'usually, a person, human being. That's what I start with. I can't think in abstract terms too much. I write to hear people on stage.'[5]

In regard to the context of the play, Miller declared:

> It was just after the war. A boom was just starting, and here I'm writing about this great war effort that we had just come through, where everybody is celebrating everything. And what the play is doing is saying, "Listen, there's a lot of crookedness in this war. There are a lot of selfish people who didn't give a damn about whether we won or lost." But What is precious, and immortal, is the connection between people, and when that is fractured and broken, the catastrophe begins![6]

According to Bob, Mary was also involved in the development of the play: 'She had a big part in it. I think she read it. I know that he sent her all his stuff, and I know that she was tough. She would speak her mind, and speak up about it, and I think it probably served him well.'

During one performance of *All My Sons*, Miller recalled: 'One tall and dignified man, I saw standing in the lobby crowd at the intermission, his eyes red with weeping.' The man was clearly overcome with emotion at what he had seen. 'Once I got the first inkling that others were reached by what I wrote, an assumption arose that some kind of public business was happening inside me.' In other words, he was gratified that his audiences were moved by the play.

The play was directed by Greek/US director, producer, writer and actor Elia Kazan, who, according to Miller:

> worked the play like a piece of music that had to be sustained here and hushed there. We were very close. He was a wonderful director. I think he was the best realistic director we've ever had. We had the same attitude

towards the theatre, which was that it was a means to expression of a world view of one kind or another.

All My Sons was an instant success and won Miller his first (of three) 'Tony' awards. Miller was also awarded the New York Drama Critics Circle Award for the best play (1946–47) by an American playwright.[7]

1946/47 was a busy time for the Miller family; In 1946, Miller's sister Joan married engineer and inventor George J. Kupchik of Manhattan. Joan became a theatre actress and adopted the stage name 'Joan Copeland'. She also had a career in television and in films. Then, in 1947, the Millers relocated to a farmhouse set in forty-four acres of land in Welton Road, Roxbury, Connecticut – an eighty-five-mile car journey from Broadway. Consequently, Miller also acquired 31 Grace Court, a four-storey house in Brooklyn Heights (which he owned until 1951), as he needed a 'pad' near to Broadway.

Also 1947, Miller wrote a screenplay called *The Hook* which, he said, was 'about the corruption on Brooklyn Waterfront [East River, Brooklyn, New York City, a commercial shipping terminal (now Brooklyn Bridge Park)], where I spent some time'.

In writer and Puritan preacher John Bunyan's Christian allegory *The Pilgrim's Progress* (composed 1667 to 1668) there is a character called 'Mr Valiant for Truth', renowned for his outstanding courage and determination. Miller, for whom this name would also have been appropriate, would undoubtedly have been familiar with this work by Bunyan. However, whereas *The Pilgrims Progress* was published in Bunyan's lifetime (he died in 1688), for Miller, getting *The Hook* produced in his lifetime was to prove impossible. (It finally premiered at The Royal and Derngate Theatre, Northampton, UK, on 9 June 2015 – a decade after Miller's death. US television journalist Charlie Rose once asked Miller what had gone wrong: 'Well,' answered Miller, 'we ran into the Cold War.'

Harry Cohn, co-founder, president and production director of Columbia Pictures Corporation 'wanted very much' to produce the screenplay, Miller explained, 'because Kazan was the director he wanted in his employ'. However, Cohn:

> got nervous, because the whole Red Scare [widespread fear in the USA over the perceived threat posed by communists during the Cold War] was starting. So, he brought in the FBI to read the script ... and worse than that, the head of the unions in the movie industry.

This was US trade union leader Roy Brewin, who was prominently involved in anti-communist activities during the 1940s and 1950s. Brewin 'was a buddy of the head of the union in New York on the Waterfront'. Clearly the US authorities were anxious to avoid giving offence to US trade unionists, at a time of geopolitical tension with the Soviets.

The outcome was, in respect of his play *The Hook*, that the FBI and Brewin 'managed to kill the whole thing'.[8]

Chapter 6

Married Life: Miller as a Father: Miller in Psychoanalysis

A home movie filmed in 1944 reveals a loving family, with Mary stroking her husband's head and Miller himself cradling his baby Jane, while at the same time dropping a shell into a stream to make a splash and thereby amuse her. 'I enjoyed being a father,' said Miller, and then mischievously, 'I also enjoyed escaping being a father!' By this, he meant escaping in order to be able to write.

According to Bob, Miller was extremely industrious, and through the years it was really a question of 'trying to catch him when he had some time to spend time'. What was he doing? 'What he always did. He was writing. At these times, we tippy toed around the studio and we could hear the [typewriter] keys clacking, and you knew you could not go in there.'

Miller admitted that he was somewhat conflicted in regard to his dual role:

> I was always in and out of my skin because I just couldn't
> be a father 24 hours a day and still do what I was thinking
> I had to do. I mean, my mind would go off in whatever
> direction it was going and then you'd say, "Oh my God!
> I forgot to pick up my son who was standing on a corner".

Bob went on to become a film producer and director. He reflected on the relationship with his father:

35

I don't think he ever really understood me in a way that he felt he could have been of much help. As we were getting to a place where we maybe could have had a constructive father-son relationship, it was the same time when the generations were getting further and further apart. So, I was obviously having to go where the energy was, for me, which was into the counterculture and he couldn't go there. And so, in some ways, it was manifested in the relationship, he kind of was dismayed by it all.

Miller's daughter Rebecca became an actor, director and screenwriter; 'When I was growing up, he continued to write, but his life had become much less public, much more private. I think he might have been sheltering himself with his family.'

She asked her father, 'Was it harder to be a daughter or a son?' He replied: 'My own view is that it's harder to be a son, because there's a certain competition going on. It's inevitable. I mean, you watch the animal kingdom, the most dangerous person or animal to the young male is his father.'[1]

The relationship between fathers and sons was something which Miller would always find intriguing. As regards children, he said, 'We cover them with myth. The parent is always a mythological figure. It's the basis of all mythology, after all. I was Zeus. You know, he's a father. He's the guy who throws the thunderbolt, kills you or raises you up into glory.'[2] Surely Miller would have preferred the latter definition!

Miller in psychoanalysis

Sadly, all was not well in the Miller household. Miller was interviewed by US journalist and media personality Mike Wallace In 1987, who said to him, 'I hadn't realised till I read the book [*Death of a Salesman*] that you were in psychoanalysis for some time.'

In fact, it was in the early 1950s, during his marriage to Mary, that Miller had commenced a course of psychoanalysis with Rudolph Loewenstein. Loewenstein was born to a Jewish family in Łódź, Poland. From 1925 he practised psychoanalysis in Paris. In 1930 he became a French citizen, and in 1939 he was mobilised as a doctor in the French army. After the Franco-German Armistice (22 June 1940), he fled to southern France. In 1942 he relocated to the USA and settled in New York.

When Wallace asked the reason for Miller turning to psychoanalysis, he replied:

> My marriage. The fact that I was unhappy. And I thought that it [psychoanalysis] would teach me something that I didn't know, about how to live. Well, it really didn't. It just illuminated the fact that I didn't know how to live. And that, I could have told you in the first place.[3]

In his autobiography Miller affirmed that he 'had entered analysis in order to save a marriage'. In other words, his marriage to Mary.[4]

Talking to Mike Wallace, Miller revealed what had attracted Mary and he to one other: 'We wanted something, each one from the other. We were mysteries to each other. She wanted the experience of the intellectual, the Jew, the artist, and I wanted America; something beyond New York.' But subsequently, 'I felt with my wife then, it wasn't enough for me, suddenly. I had a feeling that we were not close. We were not one. I had outgrown her.'

Miller, however, was disillusioned with his psychoanalyst:

> My argument with so much psychoanalysis is the preconception that suffering is a mistake, or a sign of weakness or, a sign even of illness. In fact, possibly the greatest truths we know have come out of people's suffering. That the problem is not to undo suffering, or to

wipe it off the face of the Earth, but to make it inform our lives, instead of trying to cure ourselves of it constantly, and avoid anything but that lobotomised sense of what they call 'happiness'.

There's too much of an attempt, it seems to me, to think in terms of controlling man, rather than freeing him; of defining him, rather than letting him go. and it's part of the whole ideology of this age, which is power mad.[5]

Chapter 7

Ezra Pound and Ernie Pyle

At first glance, it seems strange to mention US poet and critic Ezra Pound and Pulitzer Prize-winning US journalist and war correspondent Ernest Taylor Pyle in the same breath, for as far as the well-being of the USA was concerned, they were at opposite ends of the spectrum. But what they had in common, was that Miller wrote an article on each of them in the year 1945. These two articles are important because they reveal a) the sort of person whose beliefs and actions he admired, and b), the sort of person whose beliefs and actions he utterly loathed and despised.

New Masses was a US Marxist magazine, closely associated with the US Communist Party. Miller was theatre critic for *New Masses* from 1945 to 1946. In the 25 December 1945 issue, Miller was one of five writers who contributed to an article entitled, 'Should Ezra Pound be Shot? Five Writers Indict Him as a Traitor'. The other four writers were Lion Feuchtwanger (German-Jewish novelist and playwright); Albert Maltz (US playwright, fiction writer, and screenwriter); Eda Lou Walton (US poet and academic); and Norman Rosten (US poet, playwright, and novelist. (Incidentally, among the contributing editors to *New Masses* at that time were US poet and writer, Joy Davidman; Chilean poet, diplomat and politician, Pablo Neruda; and US base baritone concert artist and stage and film actor, Paul Robeson.)

Ezra Pound was born in Hailey, Idaho on 30 October 1885. In 1924 he relocated to Italy, where he embraced the fascism of Italian prime minister Benito Mussolini. During the Second World War, Pound was paid by the Italian government to make radio broadcasts (from 1941 to 1943) criticising the USA, President Roosevelt, and the Jews. Pound held that the cause of the war was international capitalism and usury (the practice of lending money at unreasonably high rates of interest[1]).

In May 1945, Pound was apprehended by Italian partisans and handed over to US forces. On 26 November 1945, having been returned to the USA, Pound was indicted for treason. However, he underwent a psychiatric examination and was adjudged mentally unfit to stand trial. In December 1945, the 60-year-old Pound was admitted to the Saint Elizabeth's Hospital for the Criminally Insane in Washington D.C. Here he remained for the next twelve years. Pound died on 1 November 1972.

In his article, Miller began by dismissing the excuses that had been made for Pound: that 'propaganda for fascism was undangerous'; that 'every artist's illimitable country is himself'; that Pound 'merely betrayed a particular society of men, for man in the abstract'; that Pound's propaganda was 'far too old and literary to have had an effect'. Miller also abhorred the fact that Pound's supporters 'even go so far as to advance the astonishing thesis that the laws punishing treason cannot apply to poets'.

Said Miller:

> I used to listen, now and then, to Ezra Pound sending [broadcasting] from Europe, and I can tell Mr Matthiessen [US literary critic Francis Otto Matthiessen] that, in his wildest moments of human vilification, Hitler never approached our Ezra.
>
> For sheer obscenity, Ezra took the cake. But more, he knew all America's weaknesses and he played them as expertly as Goebbels ever did. He was neither 'odd' nor 'literary'. His stuff was straight fascism with all the anti-Semitism, antiforeignism included.

According to Miller, 'The case against Mr Pound is a public and political one. He was the poet's representative and he cheapened us. Because he was a poet, his crime is millionfold. Because he was a traitor, he should be shot'. Miller pointed out that the fascists had 'murdered the great people's poet Federico Garcia Lorca in Spain, without cause, and here we have the spectacle of American writers becoming apologetic for a known and proved fascist propagandist.'[2]

The 15 May 1945 issue of *New Masses* also contained an article by Miller, entitled 'Ernie Pyle: GI'. Ernest Taylor Pyle was born in Dana, Indiana, on 3 August 1900. In 1940 he went to London where, as a journalist and war correspondent, he covered the Battle of Britain. In late 1942 he travelled to North Africa with the US military and covered the desert campaign. In January 1945 he travelled to the Asia-Pacific theatre. Miller described Pyle as having written 'the most accurate picture of Americans in war'. This was both as a journalist, as a war correspondent, and also in his two books, *Here Is Your War*, and *Brave Men*.

What endeared Pyle to Miller was that 'he understood in peacetime, that the life of a man is made up of details, and he could build a [newspaper] column on a thumbtack [drawing pin]'. Miller went on: 'He cared, he really cared. The human being was a sacred thing to him. His love for the human race was always operating and I think it is really why people loved his work.' The last time Miller saw Pyle was when the war correspondent left for Italy, after the Africa campaign.

Miller described how Pyle changed his views as the war progressed:

> I think it fair to say, that for a long time, he did not emotionally condemn the German soldier as an evil quantity in the world. He hated war and he hated whatever it was that had brought the war, but in the enemy soldier he could not find that thing. More than once he said that when you saw Nazis in the prisoners' cage you realize that they were just guys.

41

However, 'it was typical of his ability to learn from experience', because by the time of the Normandy invasion (commenced D-Day, 6 June 1944), and even prior to that, towards the end of the Allied beachhead invasion of Italy (3–17 September 1943), Pyle: 'had changed his mind. For he had seen the Nazis closer to home, and closer to home they were bombing our hospitals.'

Miller remembered telling Pyle that his play, *The Man Who Had All The Luck* was:

> about a man who kept getting everything he wanted, and never could understand what he had, or what his spirit possessed that he should deserve all he had gained. Ernie listened for half an hour, and when I was done, he asked, 'Where did you get that story?' I told him it was a fiction, and he said, 'Jesus, that's my life'.

'Other writers, such as Steinbeck,' said Miller, although they possessed 'more literary technique', never approached Pyle's reproduction of objective truth. It was because Ernie knew life and it's terrible fragmentation, and cared for it more than he knew, or cared for the rounded and interpretative forms of art. He was a reporter, and he knew what he could attain, and like anyone who does a thing perfectly, his creation became greater than itself, embodying a beauty that is the first truth of the highest art.'

On 18 August 1945, on the small island of Le Shima (now Iejima), in the Japanese archipelago of Okinawa in the East China Sea, Pyle was hit by enemy machine-gun fire and killed.

Miller did Pyle the honour of preparing 'the preliminary material' for a film which was to be 'based on Ernie Pyle's writings'. Entitled *The Story of G.I. Joe*, the film was released on 18 June 1945. Finally: 'the notes Mr Miller took at Army training camps and hospitals for this film formed the basis of his book, *Situation Normal*' (published 1944).[3]

Chapter 8

Death of a Salesman (1949)

Miller's play, *Death of a Salesman* premiered at the Morosco Theatre on Broadway on 10 February 1949. The theme of the play revolves around 'Willy Loman', the protagonist, who is unable to achieve 'The American Dream', and of how this, for him, has disastrous consequences. When Mike Wallace asked how long Miller had been formulating the ideas for *Death of a Salesman*, he replied: 'Probably all my life'.[1]

In respect of Willy Loman, he said poignantly: 'The law of success is simply that if you fail you're dead, and you are weighed upon that scale, totally, the way God used to weigh people in the old days.' (In ancient Greece, a belief was, that the soul of a person was weighed before or after death in order to decide his or her fate.)[2]

Miller was interested in:

> [what Willy Loman's] world and what his life had left him with. What had it done to him? You know, a guy can't make a living and [if] he loses his dignity, he loses his male force, and so you tend to make up for it by telling him he's OK anyway. Or else you turn your back on him and leave.

Neither of these two courses of action, of course, solves the problem. This was a theme to which Miller often returned: that of a person struggling in a world where powerful and 'impersonal forces' beyond his knowledge and control are in operation.[3]

When it came to writing the play: 'In reality, all I had was the first two lines, "It's all right, I came back". Further than that I dared not, would not, venture until I could sit in a completed studio, four walls, two windows, a floor, a roof, and a door.'

Here, Miller was referring to a single-room hut which, as a consummately gifted craftsman and handyman, he had constructed himself out of timber: 'When I closed in the roof it was a miracle, as though I had mastered the rain and cooled the sun, and all the while afraid I would never be able to penetrate past those first two lines.'[4]

Film footage exists showing the hut, approximately 12ft by 10ft, with a large window at the front and a smaller window at the side, complete with rattan blinds. The walls were clinker-built (i.e. with overlapping timber planks), and the roof was pitched. And there is Miller himself, sitting contentedly outside the hut with cigarette in hand, or sometimes smoking his briar pipe; driving his tractor across the field; or sitting inside, talking on the telephone with a beaming smile on his face and one foot on the desk beside his beloved typewriter. He was a recipient of good news, on that occasion, obviously!

In his autobiography, *Timebends*, Miller recalled:

> I wrote all day until dark, and then I had dinner and went back and wrote until some hour in the darkness between midnight and four. When I lay down to sleep, I realised I had been weeping – my eyes still burned and my throat was sore from talking it all out and shouting and laughing.

And by the next morning, he had completed the First Act, of two.[5]

This statement by Miller is extremely revealing, because it shows him to be a man of deep feeling and emotion and this, of course, is what made him such a brilliant writer and playwright.

'It would take some six more weeks to complete Act II,' he said. 'I did not move far from the phone for two days after sending the script to Elia Kazan. At the end of the second silent day I would have accepted his calling to tell me that it was an impenetrable, unstageable piece of wreckage.' However, Kazan allayed his fears, saying: 'I've read your play. My God, it's so sad!' But nonetheless, 'It's a great play Arty [Arthur]. I wanna do it in the fall or winter.'

In the play it is implied, though not specifically stated, that Willie Loman has committed suicide. This led Miller, in retrospect, to ask himself, where was 'God' in all this, and was there any 'order in the invisible world'? If there was, he said, 'I don't think I found it'.[6]

The events of the opening night of *Death of a Salesman* left Miller in no doubt that he had got his message across to his audience, many of whom, in all probability, knew just how difficult it was to achieve the 'American Dream':

> There was no applause at the final curtain of the first performance. Strange things began to go on in the audience. With the curtain down, some people stood to put their coats on, and then sat again. Some, especially men, were bent forward covering their faces, and others were openly weeping. People crossed the theatre to stand quietly talking with one another. It seemed forever, before someone remembered to applaud. and then there was no end to it.

When asked whether he was criticising the American Dream of the acquisition of money and glamour, underpinned by religion in his play, or simply commentating on the embracing of such 'values', Miller's reply was devastating: 'I'm criticising them in a sense that I think I've seen where they are destructive. In other words, people feel like failures, and then give over their lives to the idea of failure because of the fact that they haven't succeeded in the marketplace, or wherever.' Furthermore, in his opinion, people would be better able to manage: 'if they ceased measuring themselves so often and so deeply by what people think of them. That's a waste of time.'

To summarise, Miller believed that those who had failed to achieve the American Dream felt worthless, were filled with self-doubt, and asked themselves, 'Why did I go down the wrong road?' In his opinion, that was 'the kind of thinking' that could 'destroy somebody'.

What was Miller's motivation in writing *Death of a Salesman*, and did the play contain any positive message? Yes, this was a tragic play, Miller agreed. However, tragedy: 'means an ultimate confrontation with reality ... and that means that the individual and the audience gets a firmer grip on what's really going on in their society at any one time, and that should strengthen them to confront their lives.' In other words, to recognise the problem is half the battle won.

Had the success of the play affected Miller personally, he was asked by UK author, parliamentarian and broadcaster Melvyn Bragg, who interviewed him in November 1980? 'Yes', he replied:

> With a success like that you get feelings of omnipotence.
> A little touch of it you know, you think you can do anything.
> You inevitably begin to feel a kind of impact of power,
> which is sexual, it is financial, it is everything. You begin
> to shift and change, if you're not careful, which I wasn't.
> People now were talking to me differently. Women, men,
> they would look at me like an icon of some kind.[7]

To be able to share his innermost emotions with his audience was his ambition, and having done so, his success acted like something akin to an aphrodisiac!

For *Death of a Salesman*, Miller was awarded the 1949 Pulitzer Prize, for outstanding achievements in journalism, literature, and musical composition in the USA. He was also awarded the 1949 New York Drama Critics Circle Award, an annual award founded in 1935, to recognise 'Excellence on Broadway'. Finally, he also won his second Tony award.

On 29 March 1983, *Death of a Salesman* premiered in China with Miller himself as director. He revealed his knowledge of that country's history when he said: 'You know, the Chinese invented the family, the whole idea that the family was the centre of the world. They also invented business.'

People said about *Death of a Salesman* that the Chinese were:

> never going to understand it – indeed, at the American Embassy at that time, most of them said, 'They're never going to get this, you know, they're very primitive, the audience.' Except one guy, who was the political officer. His job was to understand the politics of China. And he took me aside, and he said, 'Don't worry about it for one minute. They'll get it. There's nothing in here they won't get'.

The outcome was, said Miller, that even though 'the style of the play was completely strange to them, once they got past that, they got it'.[8]

On the home front, however, all was not well, and Miller was becoming further and further estranged from his wife, Mary: 'I felt with my life then, it wasn't enough for me, suddenly. I thought I had a feeling that we were not close, that we were not one.'[9] And in his journal entry for January 1951, he contrasted 'the feeling' that he had for US actress, model, and singer, Marilyn Monroe (b. 1 June 1926), who Miller had met in that same month, with the fact that, in his words, 'I rarely see her [Mary's] face, rarely sense her. At the moment, I fear to go home.'[10] Miller's meeting with Marilyn was to have important consequences for them both, as will shortly be seen.

Chapter 9

Miller's Uncle Emmanuel ('Manny') Newman

Miller had commenced writing *Death of a Salesman* in April 1948. However, the idea for the play originated in 1947. As with so many of Miller's plays, the inspiration for them came from profound personal experiences, in this case, from a tragedy in his own family. Said Miller, 'Willy Loman' the play's protagonist:

> was based originally, on an uncle of mine who was a salesman, who was completely crazy, and he would sweep you away with these imaginary situations. He used to sit in his garage and hanging up right over his head was this spade, and I said, 'Could I borrow this spade for an hour or two?' He'd look up and say, 'I don't have a spade', [and he dared not say] 'Well, there's one right over your head!' But it was more than that. He had a tragic aspect to him, always, to me. In all his exaggerations there was a striving underneath to do something wonderful, something extraordinary, like a bit of an artist in there.[1]

The uncle to whom Miller referred was Emmanuel ('Manny') Newman (b. 24 December 1884). Newman was married to Miller's aunt, Anna (b. c.1886, sister of his mother, Augusta).

US theatre critic, John Henry Lahr (b. 12 July 1941) was the senior drama critic at *The New Yorker* magazine from 1992 to 2013. In 1999, Lahr interviewed Miller at his home in Roxbury, Connecticut.

'Manny' Newman had died in 1947, a year prior to Miller starting work on the play. His uncle, Miller explained to Lahr, had been: 'living in two places at the same time. And I thought, wouldn't it be marvellous to be able to do a play where somebody is in two or three different places concurrently. That's when the penny dropped.'

> Manny lived in his own mind all the time. He never got out of it. Everything he said was totally unexpected. People regarded him as a kind of strange, completely untruthful personality. Very charming. I thought of him as a kind of wonderful inventor. For example, at will, he would suddenly say, 'That's a lovely suit you have on.' And for no reason at all, he'd say, 'Three hundred dollars.' Now, everybody knew he never paid three hundred dollars for a suit in those days.

Miller told Lahr that 'There was something in him [Newman] which was terribly moving. It was very moving, because his suffering was right on his skin, you see.' 'What was the suffering you saw that you wanted to dramatize?' Lahr enquired. Miller replied: 'Failure in the face of surrounding success.' In other words, Newman had failed whereas others around him had succeeded.

> He was the ultimate climber up the ladder who was constantly being stepped on. His fingers were being stepped on by those climbing past him. My empathy for him was immense. And I mean, how could he possibly have succeeded? There was no way. Excepting that he'd been a pretty decent salesman in his young years. You know, he brought home enough money to raise a family of several boys. He had two daughters as well. And they lived reasonably well …. He committed suicide. That helped confirm my feeling that this man was always half in darkness. The darkness split him in half. The play was basically looking from the edge of the grave at life.[2]

No wonder Miller was so appalled by US society, and the rat race, and the devastation caused to those who, despite their best efforts, were left behind. But most shocking of all was that, like Willy Loman in his play, his Uncle Manny Newman had killed himself – hence the title of Miller's play, *Death of a Salesman.*

Who was Manny Newman in reality? The 1930 US Federal Census shows Emmanuel Newman, 46, residing at 1419 East 4 Street, Brooklyn, Kings, New York. Newman's 'Birthplace' was given as 'Poland'; 'Occupation' – 'Common Traveller'; 'Industry' – 'Ladies Dress H[?]'; 'Wage or Salary Worker – Yes'; 'Ability to Read and Write' – 'Yes'. Residing with him was his wife Anna – '44, Birthplace Austria'; 'Daughter' – 'Isabella, 21, stenographer, stock exchange'; 'Sons' – 'Nathaniel, 17', and 'Abner, 15'; 'Daughter' – 'Marjorie, 12'. All the children were born in New York City. The record also states that Newman was aged 23 at the time of his marriage, indicating that was married to Anna in 1907. Also, that he owned his house.

What were the circumstances of Newman's death? Newman's death certificate, issued by the Bureau for Records, Department of Health, Kings, Brooklyn is most revealing. His 'Address' was again given as 1419 East 4 Street, Brooklyn, New York; 'Marital Status' – 'Married', Husband of Anna'; 'Name of Father of Deceased' – 'Nathan'; 'Birthplace of Father' – 'Russia'; 'Maiden Name of Mother of Deceased' – 'Lena Budnick'; 'Birthplace of Mother' – 'Russia'.

The date and hour of death was given as '23 April 1947, A.M.'; 'Place of Burial or Cremation' – 'Bayside Cemetery'. This is the Jewish cemetery, located at Ozone Park, Queens, New York.

But what is shocking, is the following statement by the Chief Medical Examiner:

> I examined the body and investigated the circumstances
> of this death, and I further certify from this investigation
> and examination … that, in my opinion, death occurred
> on the date and at the hour stated above, and resulted from

(suicide), and … that the cause of death was Illuminating gas poisoning.[3]

Illuminating gas was a mixture of various combustible gases including hydrogen and carbon monoxide and used for lighting. Its poisonous effects are largely due to carbon monoxide.

Furthermore, on the second page of the death certificate, after the words 'Illuminating gas poisoning' were written the words 'I jet & tube'. This implies that Newman had connected a piece of tubing with a nozzle, to the gas pipe which supplied one of the gas lamps in his property.

At the end of Act Two of *Death of a Salesman*, the play reaches its dreadful climax (Miller's instructions in italics):

> *There is the sound of a car starting and moving away at full speed.* [This is the funeral hearse, containing Willy Loman.] *As the car speeds off the music crashes down in a frenzy of sound, which becomes the soft pulsation of a single 'cello string. BIFF* [Loman's son] *slowly returns to his bedroom. He and HAPPY* [Loman's other son] *gravely don their jackets. LINDA* [Loman's wife] *slowly walks out of her room. The music has developed into a dead march* [i.e. a funeral march]. *The leaves of day are appearing over everything. CHARLEY* [a neighbour] *and BERNARD* [Charley's son], *sombrely dressed, appear and knock on the kitchen door. BIFF and HAPPY slowly descend the stairs to the kitchen as CHARLEY and BERNARD enter. All stop a moment when LINDA, in clothes of mourning, bearing a little bunch of roses, comes through the draped doorway into the kitchen. She goes to CHARLEY and takes his arm. Now all move towards the audience, through the wall-line of the kitchen. At the limit of the apron* [projecting strip of the stage], *LINDA lays down the flowers, kneels, and sits back on her heels. All stare down at the grave.*

From this it is clear that Loman has died, though the circumstances of his death are not elaborated upon. However, the inference is obvious. He had been contemplating suicide and had hoped that the insurance money payable on his death would give his son Biff a good start in life.

Newman's death would have shocked Miller to the core, and he would have relived it over and over again, with rage at the circumstances which had driven his uncle to take his own life, and immense sorrow, as he wrote his play.

Chapter 10

The Waldorf Conference
(25–27 March 1949)

On 25 March 1949, Miller attended the Cultural and Scientific Conference for World Peace (or 'Waldorf Conference'), held at New York City's Waldorf-Astoria Hotel on Park Avenue. Here, he chaired the Arts Panel.

In attendance, as one of five delegates from the Soviet Union, was Russian composer and pianist Dmitri Shostakovich (1906–1975), this being his first visit to the USA.

Terry Klefstad, Associate Professor of Music, Belmont University School of Music, Nashville, Tennessee, recalled that speeches were made by 'cultural, scientific, and artistic delegates from various nations'. However, the conference 'was described in the popular press as pro-Communist propaganda, and protestors picketed the streets outside the Waldorf'.

> General themes in the speeches included the role of the United Nations; the dangerous nature of NATO (which excluded the U.S.S.R.); criticism of U.S. foreign policy and armament; the nature of democracy, intellectual freedom, and the general climate of fear. Most of the speakers advocated a strong government hand in building a new society and the need for centralised control, not only within nations, but also among nations.

To put matters in perspective, Klefstad continued, the conference:

> took place during the rising years of the Cold War. Two
> superpowers: the United States and the Soviet Union, were
> emerging and there was considerable tension between
> them. The past twenty years, or so, had been a time of
> instability in relations between the nations as American
> intellectuals saw the Soviet experiment as a possible
> utopia, and then became disillusioned as news of the
> Stalinist purges slowly made its way to the United States.

These were purges carried out under Joseph Stalin (1878–1953) –
leader of the Soviet Union from 1924 to his death in 1953.

Nonetheless, for Miller the notion open introducing a Soviet style
system to the USA as a means of creating a more equitable society
would have seemed attractive in the extreme. To the powers that be in
the USA of the 1940s, however, communism was a dirty word.

'The peace movement in the United States had gradually become
associated with the communist cause,' Klefstad continued, 'and
"peace" had become a metaphor for communism.'

Furthermore:

> by the late 1940s, the reputation of the American peace
> movement suffered from two problems: first, the inclusion
> of and control by communists; second, a platform that
> criticised U.S. foreign policy at a time when criticism of
> one's government was considered subversive. A report
> issued by the House Un-American Activities Committee
> in April 1951 explicitly linked the entire peace movement
> to Communists.[1]

Miller was surely correct when he stated that during the Second
World War:

there was simply no question that without Soviet
resistance, Nazism would have conquered all of Europe,
as well as Britain, with the possibility of the United States
being forced into a hands-off isolation at best; or at worst,
an initially awkward but finally, comfortable deal with
fascism – or so I thought.'

What Miller found impossible to accept was that: 'five or six years ago
these people [the Soviets] are saving us, and now they're destroying
us. There has to be some lapse of logic in this damn thing, no?'[2]
This statement by Miller implies that during the war the Soviets had
acted from altruistic reasons, whereas their primary objective was the
survival of their own country, to rid their land of the German invaders
and, in the mind of Stalin, to occupy eastern Europe!

Almost forty years later, in his autobiography *Timebends*, Miller
took a more sanguine view, declaring that 'Marxism is, in principle,
neither better nor worse than Catholicism, Buddhism, or any creed
as an aid to artistic truth-telling.'[3] As for the Waldorf Conference,
he said, 'Even now something dark and frightening shadows the
memory of that meeting nearly forty years ago.'[4] In particular, he
continued, it was: 'the memory of Shostakovich that still haunts
my mind when I think of that day – what a masquerade it all was!
As the recent campaign target of a campaign by Stalin attacking
"formalism", "cosmopolitanism", and other crimes against the
official line, he [Shostakovich] had abjectly promised to reform.'
However, thirty years would pass before the full facts of the great
Russian composer's persecution, and the manner in which his life
had been made 'a hell' by the Soviet authorities, would become fully
known, said Miller.

Despite his 'misgivings about doctrinaire Marxism' at the time
of the Waldorf Conference, Miller stated: 'it was beyond me at the
time to join the anti-Soviet crusade, especially when it seemed to
entail disowning and falsifying the American radical past, at least as

I had known and felt it.'⁵ One day soon, Miller's participation in the Waldorf Conference would come back to bite him, as he had always feared.

In 1950, when Miller's cousin Morton Miller took up residence in Goldmine Road, Roxbury, the two of them became great friends. In 1951, Miller sold 31 Grace Court in Brooklyn, and purchased 155 Willow Street, also in Brooklyn, a large, red-brick house built in the 1820s.

Chapter 11

The Crucible (1953)

As might be expected from Miller, his play *The Crucible*, which premiered at the Martin Beck (vaudeville) Theatre, New York on 22 January 1953, relates to yet another injustice, this time visited upon the innocent colonists of Massachusetts Bay, who were accused of witchcraft (the practice of magic, including the use of spells and the invocation of spirits, by witches – women believed to have evil magic powers[1]) in the year 1692, and persecuted by the authorities.

What was Miller's motivation in composing such a play? In the light of the so-called McCarthy witch hunts, which were currently taking place in the USA and in which people were being persecuted for alleged communist sympathies, he said, 'A living connection between Washington – i.e. the US Government – and the Salem witchcraft phenomenon was made in my mind.'[2] This 'is a play about power,' said Miller. It was also about 'the misuse of power'. In the play, he said: 'The central image was that of the guilt-ridden man, John Proctor who, having slept with his teenage servant girl [Abigail], watches with horror as she becomes the leader of the witch-hunting pack and points her accusing finger at the wife [Elizabeth Proctor] he has himself betrayed.'[3]

But for Miller, the play had another resonance, closer to home, for it 'reflected what I was going through in my own marriage [to his first wife, Mary] namely feelings of guilt', and of anger on both his and his wife's part. And for once in his life, Miller had every reason to feel guilty. He had abandoned his wife for Marilyn Monroe, when Mary had supported him through thick and thin, both emotionally

57

and financially, and by so doing, he was responsible for the break-up of the family.

In *The Crucible* there was a reconciliation between Elizabeth and the unfaithful John Proctor. But in Miller's own marriage to Mary, there was to be no such reconciliation. 'But I didn't get hung,' said Miller. 'It's the best way to reconcile people. You hang one of them.' And with a pause for dramatic effect, and a smile to show that he was not serious, 'or if necessary, both!' Deep down, however, Miller had a deep sense of guilt, which he described as 'Terrible'. 'It rolls all over you.'[4]

In England, a principal witch hunter was Matthew Hopkins (c.1620 – 12 August 1647). Hopkins was born in Great Wenham, Suffolk. His father, James, was a Puritan clergyman, married to Mary (née Witham). A Puritan was a member of a group of English Protestants, who regarded the Reformation of the Church under Elizabeth I as incomplete and sought to simplify and regulate forms of worship.[5]

Hopkins, whose career flourished during the time of the English Civil War (1642–1651), was a self-appointed 'Witchfinder General'. He even went so far as to write a book on the subject, entitled *The Discovery of Witches* (1647).

Those from the settlement of Salem (and district), Massachusetts, who were accused of practising witchcraft, numbered in excess of 200 people. They were tried in the town's court of Oyer and Terminer ('To Hear and To Determine', the name given to a court of criminal jurisdiction), a commission issued to judges on a circuit to hold courts. In this case, there were nine judges in all, and the outcome was that twenty people were executed.

'The hysteria in Salem,' Miller declared, 'which we were duplicating once again', had a certain similarity with current events in the USA, and 'perhaps by revealing the nature of that procedure, some light could be thrown on what we were doing to ourselves. And that is how that play came to be.'[6] In other words, Miller was asking himself, why have we not learned from past mistakes?

What did Miller mean when he described 'duplicating' the events in Salem? What he had in mind was the House Un-American Activities Committee (HUAC), and investigative committee of the US House of Representatives. It was created in 1938 to investigate alleged disloyalty and subversive activities on the part of private citizens, public employees, and organisations suspected of having Fascist or Communist ties. (The Committee was abolished in 1975.)

During the course of its incredible thirty-seven-year period of activity, the HUAC conducted no less than 332 hearings and investigations and interrogated hundreds of people. The amount of man and woman hours devoted to what Miller described as 'a 'farce', was truly mind-boggling!

Joseph R. McCarthy (1908–1957) was US Republican senator for Wisconsin from 1942 until his death in 1957. As a result of his activities the term 'McCarthyism' entered the language. This is the practice of making accusations of subversion or treason without proper regard for evidence. It was prominent in the USA during the period of the 'Red Scare' (late 1940s and 1950s).[7] However, McCarthy, who was chairman of the Government Operations Committee of the US Senate, had no direct involvement with the HUAC.

Miller's interest in witchcraft, and in particular the Salem witch-hunts, predated his interrogation by the HUAC. 'The beginning of *The Crucible*, I guess, goes back to the time I was in college, when I began to become interested in that phenomenon.'[8]

Miller found the case of Rebecca Nurse, one of the Salem accused, particularly distressing. Born in Great Yarmouth, Norfolk, England, on 21 February 1621, Rebecca was wife of farmer and landowner Francis Nurse, and mother of eight children. Rebecca:

> was renowned all over the place for being a very devout lady, and she had, which was unusual at that time, set up a charity for poor people; because unlike the usual romantic picture of New England at the time, there

were a large number of people who had neither land or a job, who were sleeping in ditches, who were outcasts, practically, because they were poor, and a lot of them were drunks, and she attempted to do something about these people. [She was a person who had] done nothing but good all her life.

When Rebecca Nurse was threatened with the noose she said: 'How may I belie myself?'[9] In other words, she refused to tell a lie, even if by doing so it would save her life. Rebecca was found guilty and hanged on 19 July 1692.

Miller had described the HUAC hearings as being a 'farce' which 'was too much to stomach'.[10] The Salem witch trials, which were also a farce, whereby those who pleaded innocent were judicially murdered. Whereas those who pleaded guilty (even though they were innocent) were spared!

The King James Bible as a basis for the persecution of so-called 'witches'

The King James Bible is an early modern English translation of the Christian Bible for the Church of England. It was commissioned in 1604 and published in 1611, its sponsor being James (1566–1625), who was King of Scotland as James VI, and King of England and Ireland as James I. The King was obsessed with demonology, demon being defined as an evil spirit or devil: a set of beliefs about a group regarded as harmful or unwelcome,[11] and he went so far as to write a book about it entitled *Demonologia*, published in three volumes in 1599.

In the King James Bible, the Book of Exodus (the second book of the Old Testament, Chapter 22, Verse 18) contains the phrase, 'Thou shalt not suffer a witch to live.' This eight-word phrase was to have dire consequences for tens of thousands of innocent people. For example, from circa 1450 to 1750, an estimated 40,000 people were executed for witchcraft in Europe and colonial America.

Origin of the Book of Exodus

The Book of Exodus is believed to have been written in the sixth century bce and revised in the fifth century bce. By tradition, its authorship was attributed to Hebrew prophet and lawgiver Moses, who is believed to have lived sometime between the fourteenth and thirteenth centuries BCE.[12]

Clearly, there is much uncertainty about both the origin, dates and authorship of Exodus. Not only that, but by the end of the nineteenth century, scholars were increasingly aware that the Pentateuch (the first five books of the Bible) contained numerous 'discrepancies' and 'inconsistencies'.[13] What is clear, however, is that the lives of the people living at that time and in the places referred to in the book were riddled with superstition, this being defined as 'an excessively credulous belief in and reverence for the supernatural'.[14]

A possible mistranslation

In respect of the phrase 'Thou shalt not suffer a witch to live', the ancient Hebrew word from Exodus, which the authors of the King James Bible translated as 'witch', was 'mekhashepha'. Although modern Hebrew defines mekhashepha as meaning 'witch', US biblical scholar and theologian Merrill F. Unger, in his book *Biblical Demonology*, identified the root of the word, 'khasheph', as meaning 'mutterings', which implies that it refers to 'witches who practiced magic using incantations and mutterings'. And, of course, there is 'good magic' and 'bad magic'. In other words, magic can be used in a beneficial way. However, UK biblical scholar Kenneth Kitchen has suggested that the root of the word means 'to cut', and therefore it 'refers to herbalists'.[15]

Finally, did the author of the Book of Exodus actually decree that witches' herbalists must be put to death? Professor Sayfullah ibn Yehud al-Isuni ibn Kushiym, of Orunmila Institute of Afrikan Esoteric Wisdom, Oyo, Nigeria has pointed out as follows. The correct translation of the Hebrew scriptural words 'Mekhashepha] lo tichayyah', 'which for centuries has been haphazardly mistranslated' is 'You shall not sustain [i.e. encourage or support]' the village magician, or alternatively, 'From sorcery [the practice of magic powers] you should not live [i.e. make a living]'. This is clearly a far more benign attitude to practitioners of magic than that adopted by the translators of the King James Bible, who chose to describe sorcerers as 'witches', and advocated their murder!

The pejorative term 'Witch'

A 'witch' is currently defined as 'a woman thought to have evil magic powers', evil being defined as 'profoundly immoral and wicked [i.e. capable of or intending to harm someone].[16]

However, as Kushiym states, the terms 'Witch', and 'Witchcraft' were, in fact, not present in the original Hebrew text. Instead, it was found that they had been 'later superimposed over scriptural translations …'. Furthermore, although men also practised magic, only the female version of k'shaphim [or khasheph] is to be found in Exodus. Why?

The introduction of the word 'witch' into the aforementioned phrase in Exodus, 'Thou shalt not suffer a witch to live' by the King James Bible's translators therefore suggests that they had an ulterior motive – i.e. to please the King. For as Kushiym points out, James was not only a sponsor of his eponymous Bible, he was also the author of the aforementioned book *Demonologia*, and a notorious witch hater, his hatred being 'based, it seems, in a large part on a supposed plot against him and his bride [Anne of Denmark].'[17]

Miller was astonished to learn that the superstitious beliefs which were widespread in the seventeenth century were still very much alive three centuries later. In 2008, Miller said:

I was in Salem six months ago because they were unveiling the model of a monument, that finally, after 300 years or whatever it was, they'd gotten around to making to the dead. And I had a press conference there, and these were people from all the big newspapers and wire services [news agencies], and I realised in talking to them, that they kept referring to them as 'witches': the idea being that you shouldn't hang witches, you shouldn't kill witches ... [Instead] you should put them in jail or exorcise them.

The astonished Miller replied:

'Well, wait a minute, these people *weren't* witches.' There was a dead silence. I said, 'These were innocent political victims of a manufactured Holocaust.' Well, I can't tell you the dislocation of the mind that occurred. And one woman, actually from the *Boston Globe*, a reporter, said, 'But do you mean there was no evil among them?' So, you see this is not a phenomenon from 1692, or 1952, or anything like it. It is *right now*.

There *were* witches. They were everywhere. Everybody knew that. If you were a Christian, you knew that there were witches because it said so in the Bible.

To Miller, the similarity between the Salem witch trials of the 1690s, and the inquisitions carried out by the HUAC (1938–69), and by its successor the House Committee on Internal Security (1969–75) was obvious: 'Someone had only to point a finger and shout "witch" in Salem in the year 1692, or "communist" in the USA in the 1950s, and everyone was instantly up in arms in horror and indignation.'[18]

In Salem, such an accuser was Thomas Putnam (1652–1699), married to Ann Putnam (née Carr), who was a witness in the Salem trials, was responsible for accusations being levelled at forty-three people; as was his daughter, also called Ann, for accusations being levelled at sixty-two people.

A judge with a conscience

Miller believed that of the nine Salem judges who had sentenced the accused 'witches' to death, one at least had acted against his conscience. This was Samuel Sewall (b. 1652 at Bishopstoke, Hampshire, England). Educated at Harvard University, Sewall was also a printer and a businessman.

'Judge Sewall became a bit of an alcoholic during this whole thing [the witch trials], and later wrote a book, in which he begged the dead to forgive him.' In 1696, Sewall made a public apology for his actions, as did Ann Putnam and the twelve jurors who had participated in the trials.

A macabre sequel: the Church's unwillingness to acknowledge the truth

Historically, church authorities had used the Bible as a pretext for witch-hunting. So, in the twentieth century, one might expect that some atonement would be made on their part. But this was not the case.

According to Miller, in 1992 subsidence was observed in the walls of the church not far from Salem. During the church's repair, eighteen bodies were discovered beneath its floor. The suspicion was that these were the victims of the Salem witch trials. However as already mentioned, the number of so-called 'witches' who were executed was twenty, and another five died in prison. Therefore, the remains of seven people were still unaccounted for. The church authorities refused to allow these bodies to be exhumed, in order that the truth be discovered.

Miller was appalled by the cruelty inflicted on the Salem victims in the name of religion. He referred to the case of Giles Corey who, in his eighty-first year, was one of them. When accused, Corey refused to enter a plea either of guilty or not guilty, even when he was 'weighted down with stones'. This was a torture in which heavy rocks were placed on a person's body until he or she either confessed or died. Corey died, on 19 September 1692. Corey's wife, Martha was also accused of witchcraft. Found guilty, she was hanged three days later, on 22 September.[19]

Was Miller right to draw a parallel between the Salem witch-hunts and the McCarthy witch-hunts? True, each were pursued with equal zeal by the authorities, but in fairness to the HUAC, there was a genuine paranoia at that time in respect of the Soviet Union and the Cold War.

Miller won his third Tony Award for *The Crucible*.

When, in 1953, the American Bar Association criticised *The Crucible* for being 'disparaging of lawyers', Miller responded as follows:

> The growing sensitivity of people to any sort of open and frank discussion of important issues is no service to civilisation, let alone law and order. I wrote a play about a man who happened to be a salesman, and several organisations of salespeople flew to arms. Now it is the lawyers. In defense of my right to speak, therefore, and to write the truth as I see it, I must insist upon the play as it stands.[20]

Surely such comments by Miller must find a resonance today, in this modern world of overweening and stifling 'political correctness'.

In 1996, forty-four years after *The Crucible* had its debut, Miller's play was made into a movie for which he himself wrote the screenplay.

Chapter 12

The House Un-American Activities Committee (HUAC)

On 21 June 1956, Miller testified before the HUAC, having been subpoenaed by the committee. In October 1947, Miller had 'added his name to an advertisement in *Variety*, protesting against the HUAC's inquiries into alleged communist subversion of Hollywood'. The advertisement read: 'We hold that these hearings are morally wrong: any investigation into the political beliefs of the individual is contrary to the basic principles of our democracy.'

By 1956 the HUAC had identified the 116 signatories of the advertisement (including Miller) as either 'out-and-out pro-communists', or as 'aiding and abetting the communist conspiracy'. But was it illegal to be a member of the Communist Party? Yes.

> The Communist Control Act of 1954 is an American law signed by President Dwight Eisenhower on August 24, 1954, that outlaws the Communist Party of the United States and criminalises membership in or support for the party or 'Communist-action' organisations ....[1]

In addition, in respect of the Waldorf Astoria Conference (March 1949) the HUAC, in its 1956 report, noted that the sponsors of the conference were 'forty-three "Hollywoodites", twenty-three of whom had been identified as members of the Communist Party, the remaining twenty having records as "collaborators"'.[2]

Was Miller himself a member of the Communist Party? This was something that he had never admitted to, neither is there any evidence for it. However, he was aware that he, and thousands of others, were under constant surveillance:

> A kind of popular fascism was developing in the United States, seriously. As we now know, the situation with the FBI and the rest of it was far worse than anybody even imagined in those times. There were spies everywhere. I found out only twenty-five years later when I got my records from the FBI that they had followed people from my house in Brooklyn. They had tailed people at a dinner party.
>
> The big switch was the turnaround vis-á-vis the Soviet Union, which had been our ally and suddenly was the enemy. And that left a whole sector of the American population high and dry because these people had been pro-Soviet, or at least pro-labour at that, and suddenly these people were regarded as traitors, treasonous.

The HUAC began to investigate communist activity in the motion picture industry. Miller: 'Actors, directors, everybody. Their careers were destroyed overnight. They wouldn't cooperate with some Indiana Republican who was hounding them. And you got the feeling once again that there was no value anywhere. That we were all the subject of big power.'[3]

The 'Indiana Republican' to whom Miller referred was William E. Jenner, Senator for Indiana, and member of the Subcommittee on Internal Security. He was a friend and follower of Senator McCarthy, and an enthusiastic practitioner of 'McCarthyism'.

The truth is that many of those who were hauled up to appear before the HUAC were among the most talented and creative people in the USA; others alongside Miller included Charlie Chaplin; Orson

Welles; musician and folklorist, Alan Lomax; Paul Robeson; and lyricist and librettist, 'Yip' Harburg. But, as Miller himself remarked, the HUAC were primarily seeking publicity and to entrap celebrities was its main aim.

Miller said that during the McCarthy period, he gave a lecture at the University of Arkansas. After the lecture, the faculty members sat around and he was asked, 'Now, what about this McCarthy?' And Miller replied, 'Well, what about him?' And members of the faculty said, 'Why is everybody so afraid of him?'.

Miller: 'McCarthy was, I thought, going to take over the government within a week, and everyone's running around terrified, in Chicago, Los Angeles, Washington.' But, having observed this lack of concern among those at the University of Arkansas, Miller was reassured, so much so that in an interview with Charlie Rose in 1992 he declared, with a broad smile on his face and a sigh of relief, 'I thought, well, this country is going to survive!'[4]

On 14 January 1952, Elia Kazan appeared before the HUAC, and was asked to 'name names' of people he knew to be members of the Communist Party. He refused. However, under pressure from Spyros P. Skouras, Greek/US motion picture pioneer and head of 20th Century Fox, who warned him that he had 'You'd better name names, or else you're never going to work in Hollywood again', Kazan changed his mind and proceeded to give the HUAC the names of eight former members of the Group Theater, a theatre collective based in New York who, he said, had been members of the Communist Party. But Miller's name was not one of them.

Miller and Kazan had worked on the aforementioned screenplay *The Hook* which, said US theatre critic, columnist and author Martin Gottfried, 'was about crime on the [Brooklyn] Waterfront', including 'labor unions on the Waterfront. In fact, they started a series of articles called "Crime on the Waterfront".' However, 'when Miller and Kazan broke up' as a result of Kazan 'naming names', 'Kazan took that script and turned it into *On the Waterfront*', the 1954 US crime drama film. When asked why Miller allowed Kazan to do this, Gottfried said that he had a theory: he thought Miller 'was terrified … because he could have been one of the names' Kazan had given to the HUAC. Gottfried concluded of Miller:

> I think he *was* a member of the [Communist] Party. I think he was afraid that Kazan was going to name him, and I think there was an agreement, whether it was actually verbalised or tacit. [If] You don't name me, I won't complain about you doing that movie.

Here, it should be pointed out that Miller never admitted to being a member of the Communist Party.

In another twist to the tale, Gottfried said that when Kazan produced Miller's screenplay, he 'turned it into a *defence* of naming names'. Whereupon:

> Miller turned around and wrote *A View from the Bridge*, in which the protagonist was an informer named Eddie Carbone, plainly a name [pseudonym] for Elia Kazan. A tragedy, after all. You know, Kazan is Greek, and this is a Greek tragedy about an informer who undid himself in betraying his own people.[5]

When Kazan named names, said Miller, 'It seemed to me to be the wrong thing to do.' However, he continued, 'I loved him. We were very close friends.' Miller was clearly conflicted in his view of Kazan, who had directed both *All My Sons* and *Death of a Salesman*. The outcome was that following the HUAC hearings, the two men did not speak to each other for a number of years.[6]

In a letter sent to Elia Kazan's wife Molly in 1952, Miller compared the activities of the HUAC with those of the Salem witch hunters. In Salem, he declared:

Indeed, there were no witches there. The point is that there are none now either. This committee's mentality, and the atmosphere which it has engendered after almost fifteen years of ceaseless propaganda, are such as to throw perfectly honest people into a kind of nameless fear which is utterly destructive of a sane order of life. [7]

Chairman of the HUAC (from January 1955 to 1963) was Democrat, Francis E. Walter, member of the US House of Representatives for Pennsylvania. According to Miller, before his appearance before the Committee in June 1956, Walter 'proposed to my lawyer, just before the hearing began, that if it could be arranged for him to take a photograph with Marilyn, he would call off the whole thing. He wanted a photograph, 'with himself in the picture. We could have aborted the whole thing in five minutes. And I didn't do it.'[8]

Chapter 13

A View from the Bridge (1955)

A View from the Bridge, a play about betrayal, premiered at the Coronet Theatre on Broadway on 9 September 1955. As Miller himself said, 'the cast of my mind is tragic, and you can't conceive of a tragedy without the idea of betrayal'. Referring to the plays of Shakespeare, he continued, 'Hamlet is betrayed by the King; Macbeth; Lear; it's all betrayal. It's implicit in the tragic idea.'

On the origin of the ideas behind *A View from the Bridge*, Miller said:

> That story was told me, when I was around the [Brooklyn] Waterfront in those days. I was told about a Waterfront longshoreman who had squealed on his family [and in consequence,] a tremendous outpouring of fury against him had forced him to leave the area. Nobody knew quite where he'd gone. He had to leave his family and he fled. In ancient times he would've gone out into the mountains; languished among the wild beasts.

Why the title *A View from the Bridge*?

> This particular area, Red Hook, on the Waterfront stands right under the Brooklyn Bridge. And it has always struck me, oddly, that here's this commuter traffic going over it night and day; people going over to nice neighbourhoods somewhere else; passing over this area where this Greek

drama was taking place, and nobody ever thought about it. Nobody ever, of course, knew about it.

Using language in his customary brilliant and imaginative manner, Miller described Red Hook as 'the slum; the gullet of New York swallowing the tonnage of the world'. He also referred to 'the petty troubles of the poor' and 'the green scent of the sea'.

Miller described how the residents of the Waterfront consisted of immigrants who had left Italy and Sicily, where they had been 'slowly starving', and arrived in the USA illegally in the 1930s. However, 'the organisation [presumably the Longshoremen's Union] protected them, in return for which they would give a piece of their pay to the organisation'. To them, 'America was all there was. America was the light, and Europe was the darkness. America was where all the action was, where the hope was, and I grew up with that. There was never any question that it was better here than it was anywhere else.'

In *A View from the Bridge*, the protagonist is 'Eddie Carbone', whose object of desire is 'Catherine', the orphaned niece of his wife Beatrice, for whom Eddie has developed a passion. On the other hand, said Miller, Carbone's 'instinctive desire is to fend off sexuality', because sexual – or any other sort of betrayal, 'menaces the whole fabric of their little society and for those who betray, such an act 'destroys their protection'. In other words, the community would shun him or her, and thereafter they would be on their own.

In his play, Miller was articulating the age-old dilemma, which crops up not only in plays, novels and poetry, but also in real life: if you fall out of love with a person and fall in love with another person, do you remain with them out of loyalty, or do you, to use Miller's phrase, 'Cross over'?

In respect of Carbone, the 'option he accepts' is 'that he is going to cross over', and in so doing, 'he's going to turn against his community'. Why? 'Because that's in him. He's revealing that it's not the community, but his own instinctive need that is the most important to him.' In other words, the powerful forces which come into play when a person falls in love are overwhelming and cannot be denied. In the play, Carbone also betrays 'two brothers, Marco and Rodolpho, who were dockworkers, to the immigration authorities'.

Even Miller, normally such a modest person, was delighted with the play. He wrote *A View from the Bridge* in 1955 or 1956, and:

> about seven years later, a marvellous production was done with [US actor and filmmaker] Robert Duvall playing 'Eddie'. I had nothing to do with the production, except that I saw it one day and I thought it was marvellous! Then I went back again, and Duvall had gone. An Italian actor had taken his place, and he told me the following story.

The Italian told Miller that in the small theatre of about 300 seats in which the play was being performed, he had noticed that one evening, when the audience had left the theatre, one man had remained and was in tears:

'The guy looked like an old Italian labourer, with his heavy shoes on and work clothes,' the Italian continued. When this happened twice more, the actor asked the man, 'Why do you keep coming back here?', and the man replied, 'Oh, I knew this family. Oh yes, they lived in the Bronx.'[1] But this was impossible, said Miller, because 'of course, I invented this family'. This is just an indication of the extraordinary manner in which Miller, as a playwright, was able to move his audiences so deeply.

On 11 June 1956, Miller and Mary were divorced. Under the terms of the divorce settlement, Mary received their Brooklyn house, 155 Willow Street, where she would continue to live with the children, Jane aged 11 and Bobby aged 9. She would also receive a portion of Miller's future earnings up until the time she remarried – which she never did. Miller was granted access to the children once a week, and every other weekend. Mary subsequently took up a post at the Northside Center for Child Development, New York, having been awarded a PhD in psychology. Meanwhile, he sold his house in Roxbury Connecticut.

Chapter 14

Marriage (2nd) to Marilyn Monroe (29 June 1956): The Vietnam War

On 21 June 1956, Miller testified before the HUAC. Eight days later, he married Marilyn Monroe.

Marilyn Monroe was born on 1 June 1926, so Miller was ten years her senior. In January 1951, having signed a new contract with 20th Century Fox, Monroe commenced work on a new film for the studio, a comedy satire titled *As Young as You Feel*, in which she had a small part. Meanwhile, Elia Kazan, who was working on his film adaptation of Tennessee Williams's play *A Streetcar Named Desire*, visited the set, accompanied by Miller.

It was Kazan who introduced Monroe to Miller; 'I was crying when he met me,' Monroe said later. 'A friend of mine had died ... [Miller] said he thought that I should act on the stage. People who were around heard him say it, and they laughed.'[1]

When Miller first met Monroe, he said, he fell 'head over heels' in love with her. How did the world view Monroe? She 'generally was thought of as being a rather light-headed, if not silly human being'.[2] She was seen as: 'some kind of a dancing bear. That she shouldn't be able, for example, to have any interest in anything but sex, showing off, or saying dopey things to the newspapers.'[3]

Miller, however, who was more insightful, declared: 'I took her at her own evaluation, which very few people did. I thought she was a very serious girl ... and that she was struggling ....'And unlike many others, Miller recognised Monroe's abilities: 'She was as smart as anybody. The problem with her was, that nobody could give a woman as sexy as her the credit for having any brains, in those days. She'd be much better off today.'[4]

After their first encounter, said Monroe, 'I didn't see him for about four years.' In the meantime, she hoped that Miller would notice her in one of her films. 'I can't say he gave me a feeling of security,' she declared. 'There wasn't any reason for him to really, except he treated me as a human being, and he was a very sensitive human being, and he treated me as a sensitive person also.'[5] The pair did not meet again until 1955. The following year, on 12 June 1956, Miller and Mary were divorced.

Miller stated that he had resisted getting involved with Monroe for four or five years. Why?

> Well, I was married, and I didn't want to break up my marriage. Certainly not. Since I was married and Monroe could hardly peek out of her hotel room door without being photographed, we spent much time alone together. The bond of shared silences, as mysterious as sexuality and as hard to break also began to form. After one of those silences, I said. 'You're the saddest girl I've ever met.' A smile touched her lips as she discovered the compliment that I had intended. 'You're the only one who ever said that to me.'[6]

In that year of 1955, Miller expressed his love for Monroe in a letter:

> So be my love, as you surely are. I think I shall be less furiously jealous when we have made a life together. It is just that I believe that I should really die if I ever lost you. It is as though we were born the same morning when no other life existed on this earth. Love, Art.[7]

Miller and Monroe were married on 29 June 1956 – just seventeen days after his divorce from Mary had been finalised.

Monroe's 'total honesty', said Miller, was:

> what knocked me out. She seemed utterly without guile; completely honest about herself and about anything she looked at. Whereas, the society I came from, was very guarded, judgemental. They made judgements of people. She accepted that everybody was who they were and what they were. This appearance of being absolutely free was simply a disguise. She was, in a way, the most repressed person imaginable. She had been kicked around as a child; she'd been abused as a child; she'd been deserted, abandoned. [Monroe, by her own admission, had been sexually abused as a child.] She was a very courageous human being. It was because I loved her, so I took that attitude towards her. So, the best of her, she thought, was in my eye. Therefore, the hope she had was with me.[8]

Miller was, therefore, sufficiently insightful to see Monroe for what she was, a person damaged by her upbringing, whom he would now protect and care for while she, for her part, had put her trust in him.

Miller could empathise with Monroe for the following reason. Just as he himself was an innocent, he said, so too was she. Monroe 'also, in a way, was moving in a world she knew nothing about. She was getting up in the morning, making breakfast. There was an innocence there.' On the other hand, 'She wanted to be a great star.'[9]

During this period, Monroe was a tremendous support to Miller; for example, she appeared on the steps of the Committee prior to his hearing. Film footage shows her, gracious as ever and with her unique and captivating ever-present smile, saying benignly to the adoring press, 'I would like to say that I am fully confident that in the end, my husband will win this case.' The attempts of HUAC Committee Chairman Francis E. Walter to exploit her had completely misfired.

The Vietnam War (1 November 1955 to 30 April 1975)

The two-decade long Vietnam War was fought between the communist government of North Vietnam on the one hand, and South Vietnam and it's principal ally, the USA, on the other. In respect of the war, said Miller:

'I was more of a rebel than a revolutionary in that situation. I wanted to protest but I didn't want to establish a new rule of violence. And some of them did.' In other words, some of the anti-war protesters, many of whom Miller admitted were 'very brave people', wanted to take matters into their own hands.

On 29 September 1965, Miller was invited by President Lyndon B. Johnson to the White House to witness the signing of the 'National Foundation on the Arts and Humanities Act'. The act stated that 'the arts and humanities belong to all the people of the United States'. But Miller declined the invitation in protest: 'I have very strong feelings that here we are at a crisis, where the President must act in the way that he's not acting.' I.e. act to stop what 'seems like endless war' in Vietnam. To make matters worse, funds provided for the arts and humanities under the terms of the Arts and Humanities Act were subsequently diverted in order to finance the Vietnam War.[10]

Chapter 15

Miller's Testimony to the HUAC (21 June 1956)

Prior to Miller's interrogation by the HUAC, Sue Warren was questioned. Sue, real name Susan Frank (née Heiligman), was a graduate in dramatic art from Rutgers University, New Jersey. She gave her full name as Susan Warren; address, 110 Christopher St, New York; occupation, housewife. She was shown what was alleged to be an application by Miller for membership of the Communist Party. The application form was headed 'Victory in 1943'. It also named Sue as Miller's sponsor:

Name	'Arthur Miller'.
Abode	'Roxbury, Connecticut'.
Date of birth	'17 October 1915, New York City'.
Age	'27'
Occupation	'Writer'
Present address	'18 Schermerhorn St, Brooklyn'.
Sponsor	'Sue Warren'.
	'Stuyvesant Branch, Manhattan' (12th Assembly District of the Communist Party).
Proposed by	'Sue Warren'.

There was no provision on the application form for the signature of the applicant, therefore Miller's signature did not appear on the form. The form was also undated.

When Sue was asked, was she the same 'Sue Warren' whose name appeared on the form, she courageously refused to answer any questions whatsoever, claiming the First and Fifth Amendments.[1]

The First Amendment to the United States Constitution prevents the government from making laws which regulate an establishment of religion, prohibit the free exercise of religion, or abridge the freedom of speech, the freedom of the press, the right to peaceably assemble, or the right to petition the government for redress of grievances.

The Fifth Amendment, the self-incrimination clause, provides various protections against self-incrimination, including the right of an individual not to serve as a witness in a criminal case in which they are the defendant.[2]

It was highly significant that Miller's chief interrogator at the HUAC hearing was Richard Arens, counsel for the HUAC and a former aide to Senator McCarthy himself. Miller was asked to confirm his name and address, and to give details of the educational establishments he had attended and the degrees he had obtained.

The HUAC investigation began with the issue of passport applications. On what dates had he applied for US passports? He replied in 1946 (successfully, issued 1947); in 1954 (application denied); and most recently four-and-a-half weeks ago. The 1947 passport had been obtained by Miller for a visit to Belgium and the opening of *The Crucible*. His most recent application was in order for him to visit the UK.

What was Miller's connection with the New York City Youth Board? The Board had been created in 1947 to coordinate and supplement the activities of public and private agencies devoted to serving youth. Arens' question was in regard to a proposed visit by Miller to the slum areas of New York, about which a screenplay was to be made about juvenile delinquency.

Arens pointed out that according to his passport application, signed by him in April 1947, Miller had categorically denied on oath that he: 'had been supporting the Communist cause, or contributing to it, or was under its discipline or domination'. Clearly, Arens did not believe him.

Miller was listed as being a sponsor of the World Youth Festival. This was an international event, held regularly since 1947 and organised by the World Federation of Democratic Youth. The first meeting was held that year in Prague, Czechoslovakia. Advocating democracy and opposing war and imperialism, it became an outlet for Soviet propaganda during the Cold War.

Miller was vague and non-committal in his responses. He did say, however, with scarcely veiled sarcasm, 'that in all probability I had supported criticism of the Un-American Activities Committee'.

Miller was asked when he had changed his opinion about – i.e. become disillusioned with – Marxism:

> I was not a Saul of Tarsus, walking down a road and struck
> by a bright light. It was a slow process that occurred over
> years, of really through my own work and through my
> own efforts, to understand myself and what I was trying
> to do in the world.

In respect of the Smith Act (which forbade any attempt to "advocate, abet, advise, or teach" the violent destruction of the US government), said Miller, he was 'opposed to anyone being penalised for advocating anything'.

Asked whether it was his belief that 'it is absolute that a writer must have, in order to express his heart, absolute freedom of action?' He replied: 'That would be the most desirable state of affairs. I say, yes. In the last few years, I would not participate in anything that was a Communist front of any kind.' He went on to imply that there had been a time when he *would* have participated in such activities.

Had Miller supported the China Welfare Appeal (1949)? Yes, he said, because 'there was a need for medicines and penicillin, etcetera'.

Had Miller known that Norman Rosten was a communist when he had 'collaborated with him in the play, *Listen My Children?*' In fact, Miller and Rosten had co-authored the play.

Miller was asked, 'Do you consider those things that you have written in the *New Masses* [US magazine, 1926 to 1948, which was closely associated with the Communist Party] as an exercise of your literary rights?' To this, Miller replied, 'Sir, I never advocated the overthrow of the United States Government. I want that perfectly clear.'

He was then asked whether, in 1947, he had signed a statement released by the Civil Rights Congress (a US civil rights organisation founded in 1946 and disbanded in 1956), and issued by one hundred US citizens, of whom Miller was one? The statement read: 'The Communist Party is a legal American political party. We see nothing in their programs, record, or activities, either in war or peace, to justify the enactment of the repressive legislation now being urged upon Congress in an atmosphere of an organised hysteria.'

Was it not the case that during the Second World War, US poet and critic Ezra Pound, in contrast to Miller, 'was issuing statements, and was writing plays, and issuing poems which were anti-Communist?' Miller retorted that Pound had advocated 'the destruction of the Jewish people', and that he had justified 'the cremation of Jews'. 'I felt that this man threatened me personally. I am a Jew. He was for burning Jews.'

Does the artist have 'special rights?' 'No, he doesn't,' answered Miller, 'but there is a conflict I admit. I think there is an old conflict that goes back to Socrates, between the man who is involved with ideal things and the man who has the terrible responsibility of keeping things going, protecting the state.' In other words, between an idealist and a leader who by definition must be concerned with what is possible and feasible.

Miller did admit to having been present at meetings of Communist Party writers in 1947 – 'about five or six meetings'. The meetings 'were held in someone's apartment. I don't know whose it was.'

Arens now returned to the question of whether Miller had ever made application for membership to the Communist Party.

Miller   In 1939, I believe it was, or in 1940, I went to attend a Marxist study course in my neighbourhood in Brooklyn. I signed some form or another.

Arens   That was an application for membership to the Communist Party, was it not?

Miller   I would not say that. I am here to tell you what I know.

Arens   Were you proposed for membership in the Stuyvesant Branch, 12th Assembly District of the Communist Party by Sue Warren in 1943?

Miller   I would have no knowledge of it.

Arens   Was the number on the application form 23345?

Miller   I deny it.

As already mentioned, membership of the Communist party had been made illegal in the USA two years previously, in 1954. However, from the tone of his replies, Miller clearly considered his political affiliations to be none of the HUAC's business.

Arens was not one to give up easily. He asked whether Miller attended Communist Party meetings. The answer was yes. Miller explained:

> I attended these meetings in order to locate my ideas in relation to Marxism, because I had been assailed for years by all kinds of interpretations of what communism was, what Marxism was, and I went there to discover where I stood finally and completely, and I listened and said very little, I think.'

When asked by Arens to name those in attendance at the meetings, Miller replied:

> I want you to understand that I am not protecting the Communists or the Communist Party. I am trying to, and I will protect my sense of myself. I could not use the name of another person and bring trouble on him. These were writers, poets, as far as I could see. I asked you not to ask me that question.

Arens then asked: 'Are you cognisant of the fact that your play, *The Crucible* with respect to witch-hunts in 1692, was the case history of a series of articles in the Communist press, drawing parallels to the investigation of communists and other subversives by congressional committees?' This must have been music to Miller's ear, for it was just the kind of publicity that he was looking for. Arens had played right into his hands. He replied:

> I think it was true in more than the communist press. I think it was true in the non-communist press. The comparison is inevitable, sir.

> I think it would be a disaster if the Communist Party ever took over this country. I believe in democracy, that it is the only way for myself and anybody I care about; it is the only way to live; but my criticism, such as it has been, is not to be confused with a hatred. I love this country, I think, as much as any man, and it is because I see things that I think traduce its values that I speak.

Miller was asked if he was 'more or less a dupe in joining the Communist organisations'. No, he was an adult, he said, though he did admit that he 'was looking for the world that would be perfect'. Miller was now warned that if he did not reveal the names in question, he would be in contempt of Congress. He refused, whereupon 'The House voted 373 to 9 to cite Miller for contempt'.

> Had I thought that somebody I knew was a spy or was working against the United States, that would be a different story. What are we talking about? We are talking about actors, a few playwrights, but most of them were actors, directors. What earthly effect could these people have on the security of the United States, or anything else?[3]

Perhaps the most significant statement that Miller made during the course of his interrogation was this: 'I would like to say that in those times I did support a number of things which I would not do now.'[4] Clearly, in the light of experience, he had changed his mind about communism. He was duly convicted, fined $500 and given a thirty-day suspended jail sentence.[5]

Unlike Miller, several others, as well as Kazan, had 'named names'. 'It was rather like a dream [a bad dream, obviously!]', said Miller: 'People were being torn apart, their loyalty to one another crushed, and common decency was going down the drain. And it's indescribable, really, because you've got the feeling that nothing was going to be sacred anymore.'[6]

Interestingly, it was only after his marriage to Marilyn Monroe that the HUAC became interested in him. Its committee was:

> already on a down slope. People were getting bored with them. So … they saw a terrific chance for a lot of good publicity. They went after me, primarily because I was well known and I would get them a headline in the newspaper, which is exactly what happened.[7]

During his interrogation by the HUAC, Miller displayed great resilience. When asked whether he thought the Committee's objective was to destroy him, he said 'yeah, but I knew they couldn't do that, because if I can have a piece of paper and pencil, unless they shoot me, which they weren't yet threatening to do, they couldn't destroy me because I could write plays and they can't.' In other words, Miller believed that the pen was mightier than the sword. 'Nevertheless,' he continued, the HUAC 'did destroy a lot of people who did not have that in reserve, or anything like it.'

Miller was asked whether he had ever considered emigrating: 'I never did, no. I would find it very difficult living in another country. It's hard to believe, but I love this country. It feeds me. I love to hear the language, and I'm most at home with Americans.'[8]

In a final irony, on 7 August 1958, two years after Miller's appearance before the HUAC, Washington's Court of Appeals quashed his conviction on the grounds that the questions he had been asked by the Committee had 'served no legislative purpose'.[9]

What is history's verdict on McCarthy and McCarthyism? In 1953 an official report was published entitled, 'Executive Sessions of the Senate Permanent Subcommittee on Investigations of the Committee on Government Operations'. It contained a damning indictment of the 'witch hunter in chief': 'Senator McCarthy's zeal to uncover subversion and espionage led to disturbing excesses. His browbeating tactics destroyed careers of people who were not involved in the infiltration of our government.' (The report was not published until January 2003.)[10]

Chapter 16

John Steinbeck: a Staunch Ally

One of the few people who were courageous enough to support Miller during the HUAC hearings was acquaintance and fellow writer, John Steinbeck. In defence of his friend, Steinbeck published an article in which he declared that US Congressmen:

> In their attempts to save the nation from attack … could well undermine the deep personal morality which is the nation's final defense. The Congress is truly on trial along with Arthur Miller. If I were in Arthur Miller's shoes, I do not know what I would do, but I could wish, for myself and for my children, that I would be brave enough to fortify and defend my private morality as he has. I feel profoundly that our country is better served by individual courage and morals than by the safe and public patriotism which Dr Johnson called 'the last refuge of scoundrels'.[1]
> [British writer and lexicographer Dr Samuel Johnson (1709–1784)]

In regard to Miller, Steinbeck subsequently wrote to his editor thus: 'Please give him my respect and more than that, my love.'

Steinbeck was born in Salinas, California on 27 February 1902. He was therefore thirteen years Miller's senior. Having worked as a reporter for the morning newspaper the *New York American*, he became disillusioned and returned to California, where he worked as a tour guide.

Steinbeck, like Miller, was deeply concerned with the plight of the poor and the oppressed. Miller was the playwright who cared, and Steinbeck was the novelist who cared.

Steinbeck's novel, *The Grapes of Wrath* (1939) is described as a 'deeply affecting story, about the oppression of migrant workers who were fleeing from the Dust Bowl States to California [in the 1930s], struck a chord with an America reeling from the Great Depression.' 'Dust Bowl' was the name given to the prairies of the USA and Canada where vegetation was lost, and soil eroded as a result of prolonged periods of drought during the 1930s.

In a rare interview in 1952, for the radio network 'Voice of America', Steinbeck revealed his anger at the plight of those migrant workers:

> People were starving and cold and they came in their thousands to California. They met a people who were terrified of Depression and were horrified at the idea that great numbers of indigent people were being poured on them to be taken care of when there wasn't much money about. They became angry at these newcomers.

However, this was to change because:

> Gradually, through government and through the work of private citizens, agencies were set up to take care of these situations. Only then, did the anger begin to decrease and when the anger decreased, these two sides got to know each other, and they found they didn't dislike each other at all.

Many years later, it was discovered that the FBI had begun to keep a file on Steinbeck at this time.

Like Miller, Steinbeck was not merely an observer of the world's injustices. For example, in 1938:

shocked, by reports of the Nazi looting and burning of Jewish homes and synagogues in Germany, he was among a small band of writers, including [US poet, writer, critic, and satirist] Dorothy Parker, who sent a telegram to President Franklin D. Roosevelt urging him to cut all ties with Hitler. Steinbeck became a war correspondent for *The New York Herald* during the subsequent conflict, reporting from England.

Steinbeck also intervened in the field of race relations: 'He asked for his name to be taken off the screenplay for the wartime Alfred Hitchcock film *The Lifeboat*.' The film was based on a novella by Steinbeck about a group of survivors in a lifeboat who had little chance of rescue. This was 'because he was furious that the "dignified and purposeful" black character he had created had been "distorted"'.[2] Steinbeck had every right to complain because it was he who had written the script for the film, at Hitchcock's request.

Steinbeck died on 30 December 1968, at the age of 66. In 1996, the 'John Steinbeck Award' was established and entitled, 'In the Souls of the People'. This phrase comes from the author's novel, The Grapes of Wrath, 'and it speaks to the migrants' suffering, endurance, and fine-tuned humanitarian spirit. The annual Steinbeck Award recognises an artist whose work reflects a similar sense of empathy and compassion for those, who by circumstance, are on the fringes.' Steinbeck's widow, Elaine, declared that her late husband John 'would be thrilled to have Arty receive this award'.[3]

And sure enough, in 1999, thirty-one years after Steinbeck's death, Miller became the third recipient of the award.[4]

Chapter 17

The Misfits (1961)

Miller's screenplay *The Misfits* was filmed from July to 4 November 1960 and released by 20th Century Fox on 1 February 1961. He was 'deeply involved in the production,' he said, which was an ordeal which 'sucks the life out of you for, it must have been three years'. According to Miller, another reason he was so exhausted was his looming divorce from Marilyn Monroe; and a third reason, was his observation that 'the country was changing', and he 'couldn't get a grip on it'. People's sense of value had changed: 'Suddenly, we became a real consumer society, and in a very short period of time, it seemed to me, you could no longer expect people to have a social dimension to their thought. They were all just "Me, Me, Me".' Furthermore, there was 'no moral content to the whole thing', and this was 'partly reflected in *The Misfits*'.[1]

Miller had temporarily relocated to Nevada in the spring of 1956 in order to establish residency there. This in turn would enable him to divorce his wife, Mary. This time spent in Nevada had inspired him to write *The Misfits*: 'I fell in with three cowboys while I was there, and they were hunting mustang. They were warring on these beasts. When they won, they felt good, and they felt confirmed in their manhood.' But at the end of the film, US film actor Clarke 'cuts them loose' – i.e. sets the horses free, which, Miller regretfully admitted, 'didn't often happen'.[2]

Miller was always sympathetic to those on life's periphery. These people, he said:

> are wandering around in Nevada. They're either divorced,
> or they never got married, or they simply mis-fitted,

and were disconnected from anything. Pleasant people, very nice. They love to spend the day chatting; having a couple of drinks in a local bar; go for a ride; make a few dollars catching a few horses; go back to the bar. That was America in those days, to me. It was dislocated from any purpose in life. So, *The Misfits* had a certain connection with what I was feeling.[3]

With *The Misfits*, Miller portrayed: 'an attempt by people to find some way to be at home in the world. And the world is so hard, and so rejecting, that they cannot find a niche in which to call home.'[4]

Why did Miller himself feel disconnected and purposeless? Up until then, a great deal of his motivation as a playwright was the plight of those American citizens who had failed to realise the so-called 'American Dream', and of those whose lives had been destroyed by the Great Depression. Now, however, Americans were becoming increasingly prosperous and with it, selfishness was creeping in so they were no longer interested in hearing about the hardships of their forebears during the Great Depression, which was an increasingly distant and unwelcome memory, or about the current plight of those who were excluded from US society. Miller, however, was always on the side of the underdog.

Miller generously offered Monroe a part in *The Misfits*, that of 'Roslyn Tabor', a 30-year-old divorcee: 'I just thought it would be a terrific gift for her because she'd never had a part in which she was supposed to be taken seriously, and she wanted to do that.'[5]

This was the first dramatic role that Monroe had ever attempted – and its consequences would be disastrous. During the filming she lacked confidence. She felt 'terribly responsible' for the film and believed 'that she wasn't doing it well enough or that people were not giving her enough help, or whatever'.[6] The actors and film crew also had to contend with '110 degree heat some days. It was a Turkish bath up there in a dry lake.' Monroe became 'distraught, psychologically', and 'she was also in a crisis … with the way she was being managed by Paula Strasberg', a lady whose teaching methods Miller had never approved of.[7]

Although Miller was happy 'For a while', it soon transpired that Monroe had serious underlying problems. 'After a while her dependency was too much. She was ill. She was an ill woman' due to the drugs that she was taking. 'It was that kind of a dependency',[8] and the outcome was that 'she was sick a lot of the time'. Monroe's behaviour became increasingly erratic, 'so that the picture took months longer than it should have taken':[9]

> She kept being late, missing a day's work, so everybody's hanging around all day long and the esprit of everybody was non-existent, finally. Several hundred people involved, who are leaning on this fragile creature. It's a terrific pressure and the solution was all kinds of pills and alcohol. Gigantic barbiturates.
>
> They finally had to stop shooting for about ten days while she went back to Los Angeles and just recuperated. There's no explaining a person like that, terrible.

Miller clearly took this decline in Monroe's mental condition very much to heart but felt powerless to stop it. 'She finally got through the film, and it was a pretty good film. It wasn't what I'd hoped. We separated during the shooting, and she went back to California, and they starting shooting another picture for Fox that she failed to complete.'[10]

Chapter 18

Miller and Marilyn's Marriage: the Clouds Gather: Divorce

In 1987, Miller was asked, had his marriage to Marilyn Monroe seemed like an unlikely partnership? 'No, it didn't. It seemed there was an unlikely quality to it, sure, from a cultural point of view.' But:

> the very inappropriateness of our being together was to me the sign that it was appropriate, that we were two parts, however remote, of this society, of this life. [Marilyn] was sensuous and life-loving, it seemed, while in the centre of it there was a darkness and a tragedy that I didn't know the dimensions of at that time. And the same thing was true of me. So, it wasn't that crazy.[1]

As regards her life as a film star, Miller said that Monroe: 'thought, that she wanted to come out of that career that she was now restless in, and she wanted to become a real actress and she thought she could do it by going to the Actors Studio.'[2]

The Actors Studio is located in New York. Its director was Polish-born US actor, director and theatre practitioner (creator of theatrical performances) Lee Strasberg, married to actor and drama coach, Paula (née Miller).

Miller, however, believed that Strasberg was a negative influence on Monroe:

> He made people more dependent on him. There are teachers that try to teach so that the student no longer

needs them, and there is the teacher that tries to teach so
that the student can never do without him, and the second
kind, in my opinion, was Lee Strasberg.

Without Strasberg, according to Miller, Marilyn 'felt she couldn't do
anything', and she even 'had to have his wife with her on the set'.[3]

On 13 July 1956, Miller accompanied Marilyn to London, where
she was due to start filming the comedy-romance, *The Prince and
the Showgirl* (1957). On their returned to the USA in November
1956 she and Miller took up residence at their new apartment, Sutton
Place, 444 East 57th Street, Manhattan. In that same year, Miller sold
his former family home in Roxbury, and purchased Leavenworth
Homestead, 232 Tophet Road, Roxbury, with its 110 acres of land.
The couple would now divide their time between here and the East
Street apartment.

Marilyn asked US architect and interior designer, Frank Lloyd
Wright (1867–1959) – who was then 90 years of age – to design them
a new house. The plans, said Miller, included:

> a circular living room with a dropped center surrounded
> by ovoid columns of fieldstone some five feet thick, and
> a domed ceiling, the diameter no less than sixty feet,
> looking out toward the view over a swimming pool
> seventy feet long with fieldstone sides that jutted forth
> from the incline of the hill.

Miller, who had known severe poverty in his lifetime, was frugal
by nature and to have involved himself in such gross expenditure
as this would have been anathema. Furthermore, he described the
proposed new house as 'a monster of a structure', and the idea as a
'pleasure dream of Marilyn's'.[4] Finally, the couple decided instead
to modernise the existing house and build a separate studio for
Miller.

During his interview with Charlie Rose in 1992, Miller was asked if Marilyn was irresistible as a woman: 'She could be, but she was flying apart towards the end.' Was she smart? 'Well, she wasn't smart enough to survive.' Did she want power? 'She wanted to be good [a good actress].'[5]

Sadly, it soon became clear that all was not well in the Millers' 'Garden of Eden', and that Marilyn was beginning to self-destruct. Said Miller: 'She was, how can I put it? She was everything. Whatever anybody was, she had a little of it, and it was a disastrous combination of powerful impulses in every direction all within the same woman.' Asked wether there were competing demons within her, he replied 'You name it, it was there!'[6]

Miller's son Bob said of Marilyn, 'Well, she could be pleasant, and fun, and bubbly, and lovely.' But on the other hand, 'She could go places that were just … She was in pain. You could see it come over her, in a way.'[7]

Said Miller of Marilyn, 'I never saw her unhappy in a crowd, even some that ripped pieces of her clothes off as souvenirs. Her stardom was her triumph, nothing less. It was her life's achievement.'[8] However: 'The simple fact, terrible and lethal, was that no space existed between herself and this star. She was Marilyn Monroe, and that was what was killing her.' At that point, Miller did not think that his marriage to Marilyn was doomed, but he 'certainly felt that it had a chance to be'.[9] What was the nature of Marilyn's struggle?

> Basically, her struggle was a psychological struggle against abandonment, against abuse … In our terms today, she would have been thought of as an abused child. Now the psychological damage that that creates is very well known and she struggled all her lifetime, and lost, against that damage. That's fundamentally what it was.[10]

Marilyn's mother, Gladys Pearl Baker (née Monroe):

> condemned her. Her mother was mentally ill, and tried
> to destroy her at one point, and she [Marilyn] was also
> questioning a surrounding fundamentalist religion,
> which condemned exactly what she was doing, namely
> acting and being in show business. So, there was a stain
> of the illicit, and the condemnation always there at the
> same time. She was in rebellion when she acted, and she
> expected punishment as a result of it, somewhere in that
> psyche.

But despite Marilyn's overwhelming sense of insecurity, 'the great
thing about her, to me, was that the struggle was valiant. She was a
very courageous human being and she didn't give up, really, I guess,
till the end.'[11] Miller said that he tried 'to get her to see the brighter
side of things, which is just about the most thankless job you can
possibly imagine!'[12]

Of his father, Bob Miller said: 'I think he really did as much as he
was capable of doing to try to get her to chase those demons away.'[13]

When Miller was asked why he had produced so little during his
years with Marilyn, he replied, 'I guess, to be frank about it, I was
taking care of her', which was clearly a full-time job. She 'lived in
terror that she was going to be found out as a faker. That somebody
was suddenly going to stand up and make some accusations against
her.'[14]

Understandably, for a five-year period, Miller was unable to
write. 'I was too distracted,' he said.[15] In November 1960, Miller and
Monroe announced their intention to divorce. 'So, it was the end of
our marriage, but it was also a terrible physical time for her', he said.[16]
On 21 January 1961, Miller and Marilyn were granted a divorce on
the grounds of incompatibility. Shortly after, on 6 March, Miller's
mother Augusta died in Brooklyn, at the age of 69.

Fyodor Dostoevsky, 1872, by Vaisly Perov. (Tretyakov Gallery, Moscow)

UNIVERSITY OF MICHIGAN
IDENTIFICATION CARD
(Good for current college year only)
1937-1938

Signature in full
....

Ann Arbor address .... Tel. No.

Home address
....
is enrolled as a student in the University of Michigan.

Joseph W. Bursley.

Dean of Students

ARTHUR A. MILLER

Above: University of Michigan: Arthur Miller's Identity Card.

Left: Kenneth T. Rowe during a visit to Finland in 1960.

Above: SS *St Louis* and her captain, Gustav Schröder, 1930s.

Right: Elia Kazan in Bretano's Book Store, New York, 1967. Library of Congress, New York. (James Kavallines)

Arthur Miller in 1949. Photo: Bentley Historical Library, University of Michigan.

Arthur Miller: *Death of a Salesman, Penguin Modern Classics*, London, 1949.

Certificate of Death

8767

FILED

Certificate No.

1. NAME OF DECEASED **EMANUEL** **NEWMAN** 089-07-9055
(Print or typewrite)　First Name　Middle Name　Last Name　Social Security Number

PERSONAL PARTICULARS (To be filled in by Medical Examiner)	MEDICAL CERTIFICATE OF DEATH (To be filled in by Medical Examiner. See over.)

2. USUAL RESIDENCE: (a) State **New York**
(b) Co. **Kings** (c) Post Office and Zone **Brooklyn**
(d) No. **1419 East 4 St.** Ave. St.
(If in rural area, give location)
(e) Length of residence or stay in City of New York immediately prior to death **29 yrs**

3. SINGLE, MARRIED, WIDOWED, OR DIVORCED (write the word) **Married**

4. WIFE HUSBAND } of **Anna**

5. DATE OF BIRTH OF DECEDENT (Month) **December** (Day) **24** (Year) **1884**

6. AGE **62** yrs. **3** mos. If LESS than 1 day, **30** days hrs. or min.

7. A. Trade, profession, or particular kind of work done, as spinner, sawyer, bookkeeper, etc. **Salesman**
B. Industry or business in which work was done, as silk mill, sawmill, bank, own business, etc. **Dresses**

8. BIRTHPLACE OF DECEDENT: (a) State **U. S.**
(b) County
(c) City, Town or Village

9. OF WHAT COUNTRY WAS DECEDENT A CITIZEN AT TIME OF DEATH? **U. S.**

10. WAS DECEASED WAR VETERAN? IF SO, NAME WAR **no**

11. NAME OF FATHER OF DECEDENT **Nathan**

12. BIRTHPLACE OF FATHER (State or Country) **Russia**

13. MAIDEN NAME OF MOTHER OF DECEDENT **Lena Budnick**

14. BIRTHPLACE OF MOTHER (State or Country) **Russia**

15. SIGNATURE OF INFORMANT *George Karp* RELATIONSHIP TO DECEASED **son-in-law** ADDRESS **1419 E. 4 St., B'klyn**

16. PLACE OF DEATH:
(a) NEW YORK CITY: (b) Borough **Brooklyn**
(c) Name of Hospital or Institution **1419 East 4 St.**
(If not in hospital or institution, give street and number)
(d) If elsewhere than in hospital or own residence, specify character of place of death, as: hotel, office, store, street, toolcab, etc.

17. DATE AND HOUR OF DEATH (Month) **April** (Day) **23** (Year) **1947** (Hour) A M.

18. SEX **Male**　19. COLOR OR RACE **White**　20. Approximate Age **62**

21. I hereby certify (a) that in accordance with Sections 878-2.0 and 878-3.0 of the Administrative Code for the City of New York, I went to, and took charge of the dead body at **1419 East 4 St.**
this **23** day of **April** 19 **47**
(b) that I examined the body and investigated the circumstances of this death, and *(Cross out terms that do not apply.)
I further certify from the investigation, (including the body, personal physician of deceased or other) and examination (a) that, in my opinion, death occurred on the date and at the hour stated above and resulted from (accident or violence) (homicide) (suicide) and (d) that the causes of death were:

Illuminating gas poisoning

M. E. Case
Signed *[signature]* Assistant Medical Examiner
Approved *[signature]* Chief Medical Examiner
No. **1428**
Date **4/2/47**

22. PLACE OF BURIAL OR CREMATION **Bayside Cemetery** DATE OF BURIAL OR CREMATION **April 25th 1947**

23. FUNERAL DIRECTOR **Flatbush Memorial Chapel** ADDRESS **Inc 1283 Coney Island Ave** PERMIT NUMBER **2850**

BUREAU OF RECORDS AND STATISTICS—DEPARTMENT OF HEALTH—CITY OF NEW YORK

Emmanuel Newman: Death Certificate page 1. Bureau of Records, Department of Health, Kings, Brooklyn, New York.

MEDICAL EXAMINER'S SUPPLEMENTARY REPORT

Did death follow operation?........................If so, state condition for which performed:......................

....

If cause of death mentions any drug, chemical, or therapeutic procedure, state reason for its use:..................

....

(The following items are to be completed for deaths due to accident, suicide or homicide)

Date of injury....**April 23,**........19**47** Borough where injury occurred........**Brooklyn**

Where did injury occur? (Street and number)............**1419 East 4 St.**

Did injury occur: at home?..........**yes**..........................in industrial place?..................

in public place?...................................while at work?..................

Means of injury:..**Inhaled illuminating gas poisoning - 1 jet & tube**..................

....

TO FUNERAL DIRECTORS

Regulation 3, Section 46 of the Sanitary Code provides that—"No permit to remove, ship, cremate or bury the remains . . . will be issued unless the funeral director applying for such permit shall sign his name . . . and shall certify in writing that he has been employed by the nearest surviving relative or next of kin."

Caskets containing bodies of persons dead from certain communicable diseases must be permanently sealed before removal from the place of death. Section 103 of the Sanitary Code of the Board of Health requires that every undertaker engaged for, or in charge of, the preparation and burial of the body of a person who died in the City of New York from any of the following diseases: **Asiatic Cholera, Diphtheria, Meningococcus Meningitis (Epidemic Cerebrospinal Meningitis), Plague (all forms), Acute Anterior Poliomyelitis (Infantile Paralysis), Scarlet Fever (Scarlatina), Smallpox (Variola) and Typhus Fever**—shall immediately place the body in a coffin or casket and **permanently close and seal** it with seals provided for the purpose by the Department of Health.

Removal of bodies prohibited without permit. The regulations of the Board of Health prohibit the removal of the body of a human being, who died in the City of New York, unless a permit therefor has been obtained from the Department of Health, except when such removal is ordered in connection with an investigation conducted by the Office of the Chief Medical Examiner, a District Attorney or the Police Department.

Permission to remove dead bodies granted by telephone. In keeping with these regulations, the Department of Health will grant to Funeral Directors by telephone, permission for the removal of a body to a home or funeral chapel in the city, provided the application is made by a licensed Funeral Director who has the certificate of death in his possession at the time of telephoning. Such permission may be granted by the burial permit clerk in Manhattan, when the office in the borough in which the death occurred, is closed. Removal of a body before obtaining permission may be penalized by suspension of telephone removal privilege, by court action, or by revocation of business permit.

FUNERAL DIRECTOR'S CERTIFICATE

I hereby certify that I have been employed, without any solicitation on my part or that of any other person, to dispose of the remains of

............**Emanuel Newman**............

by............**Anna Newman**............of............**1419 East 4th St**............

who is the............**Wife**............and the nearest surviving relative or next of kin of the deceased.
(Relationship)

Name of permittee............**Flatbush Memorial Chapel Inc**............Permit No.....**2850**

By............*Natella Sherman*............
(Signature of licensed manager or funeral director if other than permittee)

To Be Filled in by the Funeral Director When Obtaining Removal Permit by Telephone

Telephone Removal No....**NONE**....................granted by....................
(Burial Clerk)

Date....................Hour....................(A.M.)
(P.M.)
(Funeral Director)

Emmanuel Newman: Death Certificate page 2. Bureau of Records, Department of Health, Kings, Brooklyn, New York.

Joseph R. McCarthy, 1954.
(Library of Congress)

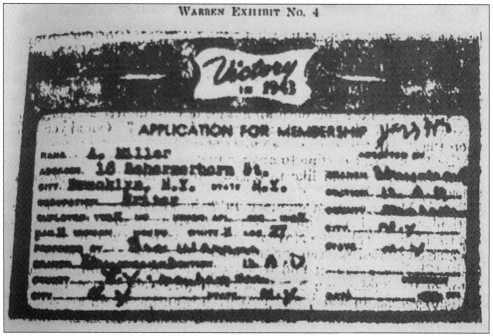

Arthur Miller's application to join the Communist Party. HUAC exhibit.

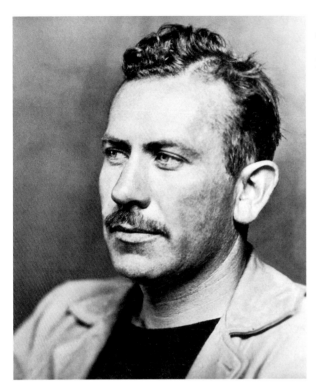

John Steinbeck, November 1939. (McFadden Publications)

Charles Chaplin.

Above: Joan Baez with Bob Dylan,
Civil Rights March on Washington
DC, 28 August 1963. (Rowland
Scherman, US Information Agency)

Right: Aleksandr Solzhenitsyn,
17 February 1974.
(Dutch National Archives)

Charles Dickens, Heritage Auction Gallery, Dallas, Texas. (Jeremiah Gurney)

Helen Muspratt, circa 1932, by Lettice Ramsay. (Jessica Sutcliffe)

Marriage of Marilyn Monroe to Arthur Miller, 29 June 1956. (from May 1962 issue of *TV-Radio Mirror*)

Inge Morath: *Her Life in Photos*.

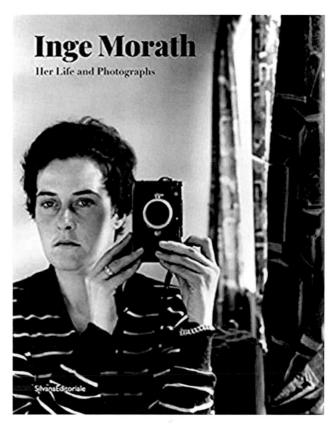

Arthur Miller in 1966.
(Dutch National Archives,
The Hague, Netherlands)

Above: Southbury Training School, Connecticut.

Left: Daniel Day-Lewis and Rebecca at the 2008 Academy Awards.

Joan Copeland at the 19th Annual Hampton's International Film Festival, New York, 16 October 2011. (Nick Stepowyj)

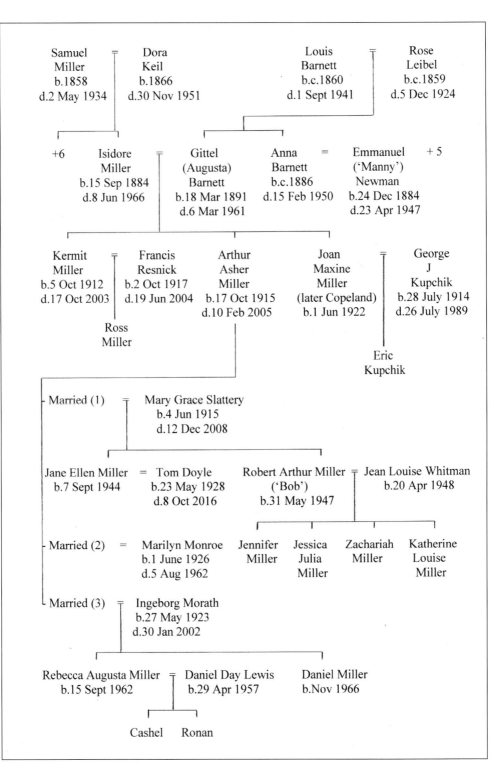

Arthur Miller family tree.

Chapter 19

The Death of Marilyn and its Effect on Miller: Ingeborg Morath

Marilyn died on 5 August 1962 at her home in Los Angeles. She was aged only 36. It was as he was completing his next play, *After the Fall*, that 'the horrifying news came that Marilyn had died, apparently of an overdose of sleeping pills'.[1] In fact, at post-mortem, an lethal quantity of barbiturate was found in Marilyn's body.

A reporter called to enquire if Miller would be attending Marilyn's funeral in California. 'The very idea of a burial was outlandish, and stunned as I was, I answered without thinking: "She won't be there".'[2]

In a handwritten essay, composed by Miller on 8 August 1962, three days after Marilyn's death, he visualised the scene at her funeral – which he did not attend.[3] Unable to conceal his bitterness at what in his opinion her associates had done to her, he imagined the 'public mourners', who:

> stand there weeping and gawking, glad that it is not you, going into the Earth. Glad that it is this lovely girl who, at last, you killed. Instead of jetting to the funeral to get my picture taken, I decided to stay home and let the public mourners finish the mockery. Not that everyone there will be false, but enough. Most of them destroyed her, ladies and gentlemen.[4]
>
> She was destroyed by many things, and some of those things are destroying you … destroying you now.

There have been many conspiracy theories about the death of Marilyn Monroe, as is always the case, but the likelihood is that she took her own life. Why, when she evidently had so much to live for? Marilyn was a gifted, intelligent and caring person, deeply sensitive and possessing a poetic soul. Her lifelong need for an 'attachment figure' – a person who would love her and upon whom she could rely absolutely – was indicative of Emotional Deprivation Disorder, stemming from her highly disrupted and insecure childhood. All her life she longed for what she had largely been deprived of as a child: true and lasting love. And it was that yearning, combined with her vulnerability, which touched the hearts of millions throughout the world.

Marilyn was also a driven person: her insecurity propelling her inexorably onwards as, terrified of failure, she strove to perfect her craft as an actress. Of course, creativity is so often forged in the crucible of pain, as Miller himself knew only too well.

Miller was consumed by grief and guilt at the news of Marilyn's death. But he was not aware, that she had a serious underlying condition, namely Borderline Personality Disorder (BPD), which held her in its grip for the whole of her all-too-short adult life. And as she ascended each rung of the ladder of success, her BPD inexorably dragged her back down into a world of morbid thoughts and 'suicidal ideation'.[5]

The various features of BPD are as follows:

1. Identity disturbance, unstable self-image; a feeling of lacking a meaningful relationship, nurturing, and support; seeing one's self as bad or evil.
2. Feelings of emptiness: a feeling that one does not actually exist.
3. Frantic efforts to avoid real or imagined abandonment.
4. Bouts of anxiety: episodic dysphoria (a state of unease or dissatisfaction).

5. Impulsivity that is potentially damaging, including substance abuse, and being spendthrift.
6. Instability in interpersonal relationships; may switch from idealising other people, to devaluing them because they do not care enough or do not give enough.
7. Inappropriate displays of anger: difficulty in controlling anger.
8. Paranoia – i.e. delusions of persecution, unwarranted jealousy, or exaggerated self-importance. Distrust and suspiciousness of others, whose motives are interpreted as malevolent.
9. Severe dissociative symptoms (feeling separate or disconnected); becoming disconnected from one's thoughts, feelings, memories, or sense of identity.
10. Recurrent Suicidal Behaviour, Gestures, or Threats: Self-Mutilating Behaviour.[6]

If BPD is the correct diagnosis, and if Marilyn experienced a range of the associated symptoms, then how could any human withstand them? It is unlikely that even a whole army of psychiatrists could have saved her. No wonder Miller was unable to help the woman he loved, and in utter despair about what he perceived as his failure in this regard.

What of the future? Surely, Miller's dream was to have a partner with whom he could share his hopes, and above all his art.

As already mentioned, although Miller's father was illiterate, his mother, Augusta, was perfectly literate and widely read. Augusta had read him stories as a boy and taught him a love and respect for books. Had such literary companionship existed in his previous marriages? Yes, in his marriage to his first wife Mary, certainly. But not to the same extent with Marilyn. However, a bright new star now appeared in the firmament in the shape of Ingeborg ('Inge') Morath, who fulfilled all these criteria admirably, and became his soulmate.

Ingeborg Hermine Morath was born in Graz, Austria, on 27 May 1923, to Edgar and Mathilde (née Wiesler) who were both scientists.

In the 1930s the family relocated to Berlin, where Inge studied languages at the city's university. Towards the end of the Second World War, Inge was drafted for factory work. When the factory was bombed by the Russians, she fled on foot to Austria. Inge subsequently worked as a translator, a journalist and finally, as a professional photographer.

According to Inge and Miller's daughter Jane, 'My mother suffered a lot during the war, and after the war she had to work in a munitions factory in Berlin. She was interrogated by Nazi officials because she wouldn't join the Hitler Youth even though her father was a member of the Nazi Party'. Inge recalled that the factory was heavily and constantly bombed, and how, when Berlin fell, she walked the 450-or-so miles from Berlin to Salzburg in neighbouring Austria: 'because there was no transport. Everyone was walking, fleeing. There were refugees and horses, all the people from the East with dead babies. It was horrible! You kind of lose your mind a little bit.'

According to Rebecca:

> As much as [Inge] was somewhat of a damaged person by that, she was also such a hugely positive dynamo of a woman. She was the first female photographer to be a full member of Magnum Photos, and really built herself a spectacular life filled with work and love affairs; a beautiful apartment, and wonderful clothes. She met Arthur and she was a very wounded person at that point.

Ingeborg, said Miller, 'was one of several photographers from Magnum Photos [founded in Paris in 1947], which is a cooperative photographic agency in New York, who was working on *The Misfits*'.[7] She subsequently spent time filming in Argentina and France. 'Then we met about a year later,' said Miller, when he was seeking photographs with which to illustrate a book that was being written about *The Misfits*. Miller and Inge were married on 17 February 1962.

100

Inge described Miller as 'a very lonely man, very lonely'. She said that when she arrived on the scene, 'there was just one or two friends. I mean nobody, nobody came. I brought in all these folks and friends, I think in many ways because he doesn't know how to reach out.' However, in regard to Miller's children by his first wife Mary, Inge said: 'I always had a very good relationship with Bobby and Jane. Yes, I saw them a lot, because I was doing something. Being a photographer was fun for them.'

Bob ('Bobby') confirmed that this was the case: 'That house was really not a real home until she came. Inge put flowers on the table; curtains on the windows; it started to feel lived in. He seemed to be refreshed and renewed and re-invigorated by it.' Delightful film footage exists, for example, of Miller helping Inge in the kitchen, and carving a chicken with a whoop and a flourish!

As regards Bobby's relationship with his father, it had not always been harmonious. Bobby reflected on growing up:

> As we were getting to a place where we could have a constructive father-son relationship, it was at the same time as the generations were getting further and further apart. [The so-called 'Generation Gap'.] So, I was obviously going to go where the energy was for me, which was into the counterculture. And he couldn't go there. It was manifested in the relationship. He kind of was dismayed by it all.

Miller and Inge proceeded to plant hundreds of 'seedlings' [trees] in their extensive grounds. A photograph exists of them standing in the snow, he in a fur-lined coat and she in a leopard-skin coat, hugging each other. Life had definitely become worth living once again!

On 15 September 1962, their daughter Rebecca was born. 'When I was born,' she said, 'my father was the one who knew more about babies. My mother picked out a baby's carriage [pram] for me which was, in fact, a doll's carriage. My father had to inform her that I needed something bigger.' When Rebecca asked her father what he thought made a good father, he replied: 'Children [are] helpless, so they create the definition of this great force, which can sweep away or comfort them.'[8]

Remembering her mother, Rebecca said: 'She used to go on trips, to photograph various things, and she would go for about two weeks.' However, 'She realised that [Miller] could stand it for two weeks, to be on his own. Then she had to come back.' In a letter to Inge during one such period of her absence, Miller revealed his vulnerability and sense of insecurity:

> Inge dear, I miss you. I am discouraged with myself, my
> rootlessness. And ashamed, too. I can't talk to anyone but
> you, about so many things. I feel haunted sometimes by
> the question of whether anything, any feeling, is eternal.
> I am done today but want to reach out my hand to you.
> Inge, come back.

As for Inge, said Rebecca: 'She believed in him enormously, she believed in his talent, and also in him as a person, and I think that he had come to a point where he felt terrible about himself. I think that she rejuvenated him.' As if to prove the point, Miller and Inge co-authored three books. They were entitled, *In Russia* (1969); *In the Country* (1977); and *Chinese Encounters* (1979).

Inge made Miller happy, and he made her equally happy. Marriage, she said: 'It's a kind of a mutual love and respect, and to be there for somebody and somebody there for you. It's wonderful!' As for Miller, in later life he described his relationship with Inge as 'an intimate coming together between two disciplines. She's just terrific, let's face it! I can say that after thirty-five years married to her. But it seems like a day.'[9]

Chapter 20

After the Fall (1964): *Incident at Vichy* (1964): *The Price* (1968): *The Creation of the World and Other Business* (1972)

After the Fall

Miller's play *After the Fall* premiered at the ANTA Washington Square Theatre on Broadway on 23 January 1964. True to form, in the play he seized on a subject of which he had profound personal experience, namely his marriage to Marilyn. 'Quentin', a lawyer, is a thinly disguised Miller, and his second wife, 'Maggie', is a thinly disguised Marilyn. And in the play, which is about the complications of interpersonal relationships in marriage, Miller dealt with precisely the same dilemma that he personally had faced in having to cope with Marilyn and be responsible for her, given her drug dependency.[1]

But how had Miller regained his creative urge? Why did he feel that he could finally create the play, having previously been distracted? Partly, of course, because he now had peace of mind with Inge, but also, as he declared, because 'I could finally confront all the contradictions in myself, and in the world that I was with.' And if writing the play would help him to identify and understand those contradictions, then this would be a catharsis – the process of releasing, and thereby providing relief from, strong or repressed emotions[2] – for him.

103

Miller based *After the Fall* on the philosophical novel, *The Fall* by French philosopher, author and journalist, Albert Camus (1913–1960).[3] In the novel, 'Jean-Baptiste Clamence', a lawyer, encounters a woman who is about to throw herself over a bridge. But he continues on his way. Then he hears a splash and prolonged screaming. But despite her screams, still he does not assist her. In respect of Clamence, Miller posed the question:

'"What if he *had* saved her?". You see I think that all suicides are murdered. They are the victims of aggression, or sometimes the victims of truth.' Here, it is difficult to escape the conclusion that Miller felt so guilty about Marilyn's death, that he actually felt he had murdered her.

In *After the Fall*, Miller changed the dynamic of Camus's novel as follows. 'It gradually began to occur to me,' he said:

> well, that's one dilemma, but supposing he [Quentin] *had* tried to save her [Maggie], and supposing he *had* saved her. He would now be confronted with the complicated human life of a woman who wanted to kill herself. What is his responsibility then? How does he relate to that responsibility? Because now, he really *has* taken on the role of the man who saved her. He has put himself in the way of God.

'In *After the Fall*,' Miller continued, 'one of the partners of this marriage cannot go forward with the illusion that the other one had. It means she dies alone, or they both go down; or whoever can save himself saves himself.'

Miller articulates the very same dilemma that he had faced with Marilyn: that of altruism versus self-preservation; 'people are far more difficult to change than I had allowed myself to believe'.

In his mind, over and over again, Miller reflected on his former role, vis-à-vis Marilyn, and he agonised over whether he could have done more to save her. But the truth was, of course, he *had* done his utmost to save her because he loved her. And yet, because of her Borderline Personality Disorder, it is doubtful whether anyone could have saved her.

In *After the Fall*, when Quentin says poignantly, 'A suicide kills two people, Maggie. That's what it's for', this implies that Marilyn had killed herself, *knowing* that her death would destroy him also. (It is, of course, highly unlikely that this thought ever crossed Marilyn's mind.) It also implies that Miller himself *had felt destroyed* by Marilyn's suicide (which is undoubtedly true), even though the couple had been divorced for eighteen months when the tragic event took place.

Another theme Miller had in mind when writing *After The Fall* was the Nazi Holocaust:

> And *After the Fall* is involved, gradually and slowly, with that idea that I extrapolated into the whole Nazi experience. Because in the interval, I went through Germany for months with Inge, and in those days, you could still walk among the concentration camps. They hadn't been cleaned up as they have been now, and the whole question of one's relationship to the destroyed, to the people who finally get it in the face, was also in that play.

After the Fall, he said, 'was an attempt to arrive at a real relationship with self-destruction'.

There were those who felt that in *After the Fall*, Miller had deliberately traded on Marilyn's suicide. This was to impugn Miller's integrity, which was beyond reproach. After all it was always his habit to make suffering, whether in himself or others, the subject of his plays.

According to Miller, the public's reaction to the play:

> was mostly ferocious .... and it blew my image away for a lot of people. They hated me. And I had rationalised

it any way as being something you deny; you deny the murderer in you. You deny the complicity with evil. That's why evil goes on. If we cease to deny it, and saw our own culpability, maybe it wouldn't be as prevalent. But that's evil. We're good, but we don't do bad things.

Miller's feelings of guilt over the death of Marilyn had evidently overwhelmed him to such an extent that he was unable to think rationally, so instead of seeing himself as someone who did everything possible to help her, he now saw himself as being complicit in her death. This is clearly a nonsensical step too far!

Miller continued:

People did not want to be confronted with what that play was saying and that play is saying that, at a certain point, you are ready to sacrifice somebody, as the Jews were sacrificed in Europe; as our 58,000 men were sacrificed in Vietnam; as who knows what, every day of the week, is not sacrificed by human beings who simply are tired of having the responsibility for them.[4]

Clearly, this was the case with Miller and Marilyn who, reading between the lines, had driven him to the point of utter exhaustion bordering on insanity.

Showing commendable insight, Rebecca concluded that 'Quentin, essentially, is trying himself [putting himself on trial] for the fact he could have killed Maggie, and in that sense, it reflects the [Miller's] relationship with Marilyn.' When asked whether this was true, Miller replied 'Yes, sure.'[5]

At about this time, said Miller, Kazan and Canadian theatre producer Robert ('Bob') Whitehead came to him seeking his support for an attempt to create an American National Theater. (Not to be confused with the American National Theater and Academy, established in 1935 as a non-profit making theatre and training organisation.) Miller readily agreed. 'This was basically why we all got together,' he said, 'because we all believed in the same thing. Kazan was head of the Lincoln Center [for the Performing Arts in the Lincoln Square neighbourhood of Manhattan] at that time.'[6]

Incident at Vichy

The origin of Miller's *Incident at Vichy* (1964) dates back to a story told to Miller by Rudolph Loewenstein, Miller's psychoanalyst from 1947 to 1949, about a Jewish psycho]analyst who was 'arrested with false papers and saved by an unknown gentile'.[7] The incident in question occurred in France when the Vichy Government came to power after that country's defeat and occupation by the Germans in the Second World War. *Incident at Vichy*, which was directed by Kazan, premiered at the ANTA Washington Square Theatre on Broadway on 3 December 1964. Miller said it:

> was an attempt to deal with what I've always felt was the most important single event in this century, and maybe ever. I think that the destruction of German culture and the transformation of that people into the barbarians that they were [under Führer Adolf Hitler] is a lesson to us all, and that this is saying to the world, 'Watch out!' These people were the most cultivated people in Europe; they were probably the best educated people in Europe; the most socially disciplined people in Europe; in many ways the most progressive people in Europe, and in the space of a couple of years they were burning people up. And you have to face this in human nature.

Once again, Miller was wrestling with the question of suffering, and its causation.

But how did this happen? asked interviewer Charlie Rose. Miller was under no illusions:

> There is in all of us a retrograde desire to kill, to destroy. A love of the dark. And we have a lot of forces that keep us from doing it most of the time. And when a leadership rises in a country, that believes that it can lead by using the darkness in man, it's probably unstoppable at a certain point.

Yet this was not a purely German phenomenon Rose pointed out, and Miller concurred: 'We've seen it in more than one place.' Was Stalin an example? Rose asked. 'Yeah. The power over others; the willingness to destroy others, is very deep in the human mind.'[8]

Miller was active on other fronts in addition to playwriting. For example, from 14–18 September 1965, an international conference was held at the University of Michigan, advertised on the programme as 'Alternative Perspectives on Vietnam: To Discuss Alternatives to US Policy in Vietnam.' The speakers included Miller; Lord Fenner Brockway, member of the British House of Lords; Makoto Oda, Japanese novelist; Emil Mazey, Secretary-Treasurer of the United Automobile Workers.

Sadly, on 1 June 1966, Miller's father, Isidore died, aged 81.

The Price

Miller described the 1960s as: 'a total upheaval, not just for me but in general, and I couldn't really satisfactorily express my sense of it at the time. The young folks were looking in an entirely different direction for their ideas and for their feelings.' In other words, in the post-war era of pop music, pop concerts, rock and roll, clubbing, the movies, fashion, etc., the new generation of the Western world was preoccupied with enjoying themselves as never before. Nonetheless, Miller continued, 'I remember I had a very successful play, *The Price*

(1968) at that time.' *The Price* premiered at the Morosco Theatre on Broadway on 7 February 1968.

The play tells the story of two brothers, Victor and Walter Franz, who, after an estrangement of sixteen years, come together again after the death of their father. Victor was the son who had abandoned his dreams of a college education in order to support his father, following the Stock Market Crash of 1929 and the death of his mother; subsequently, he has been struggling to make ends meet as a police officer. Walter, on the other hand, became a wealthy and successful surgeon, but suffered a nervous breakdown and a divorce. So, both brothers paid a price: Victor for forgoing his education, which left him bitter and resentful; and Walter, who now finds life meaningless after his frenzied but fruitless pursuit of wealth and fame.

The play is evidently reflecting Miller's feelings of guilt for going away to college and leaving his brother Kermit to try and help their father, Isidore, to save the family business. However, if any animosity had ever existed between the two brothers on this account, the warm relationship that they had now, as amply demonstrated in the film *Arthur Miller: Writer*, which Rebecca made about her father. Referring to *The Price* Miller said:

> My play was successful. It had wonderful people in it. [It was] very nicely done. But you got the feeling it didn't matter anymore. I didn't feel that there was anybody out there who was interested, and I felt that I was shouting into a barrel. You know, the game was not worth the candle. So, you made people feel this, or feel that, or laugh, or weep, so what the hell's the difference? What's the point of it all?[9]

Miller was clearly disillusioned that this play about human responsibility sounded irrelevant and old-fashioned to the new generation.

What of Kermit, who was three years Miller's senior? Kermit graduated from Madison High School, Brooklyn, in June 1930, and that autumn was admitted to New York University. (What subject Kermit was studying is not known.) However, he was obliged to leave after the first year in order to try to save the family business from bankruptcy. When that failed, he earned his living as a carpet salesman.

The Creation of the World and Other Business (1972)

Miller's play *The Creation of the World and Other Business*, which premiered at the Morosco Theatre on Broadway on 30 November 1972, is a parable in which the concepts of good and evil are explored, through a retelling of the events of the Bible's Book of Genesis. However, in *The Creation of the World and Other Business*, said Miller, 'the usual process' was reversed. 'The usual process,' he declared, is that God 'creates the people.' But 'in my play, the people are there first, and they created God, whom they proceed to obey and adorn with all kinds of powers. There had to be some kind of a moral system,' he said, otherwise it 'would be the end of the world.' This was entirely in accordance with Miller's views as an atheist.

'I thought that was interesting,' said Miller, but he discovered that his words were falling on deaf ears. 'Nobody got it. Not really, very much.'[10]

Meanwhile, having attended art school, Miller's daughter Jane chose to specialise in textiles and weaving. On 1 August 1970 she married Tom Doyle, a sculptor of Roxbury, Connecticut. On 6 August 1977, Miller's son Bob married Jean Louise Whitman (b. 20 April 1948). They had four children: Jennifer; Jessica Julia; Zachariah; and Katherine Louise.

Chapter 21

Miller at Home: Humour; Gaiety; Contentment

Drawing on material that had been collected for over thirty years, Miller's daughter, actress, director, and screenwriter Rebecca, decided to record her famous father on film. *Arthur Miller: Writer: A Film by Rebecca Miller*. Was a Round Films Production for HBO Documentary Films, and was released on 8 December 2017.

Rebecca Augusta Miller, daughter of Arthur and Inge, was born on 15 September 1962. On 13 November 1996, she married British actor Daniel Day-Lewis (they went on to have two sons, Cashel and Ronan). Said she of her father, 'I felt that I was the only film-maker that he would let close enough to really see what he was like.' In this endeavour, Rebecca was quite correct. She and her father clearly got on well, and she was gentle in her approach rather than being confrontational; as a result, Miller was relaxed and able to speak freely and often with humour. Therefore, Rebecca did not have to coax the answers out of him because they came naturally, and he answered candidly. Finally, Rebecca asked pertinent questions; sought clarification if the answers required it; and made sure that the interviews flowed smoothly and coherently. Consequently, the film was a great success.

Miller, when not appearing in a formal setting as was presently the case, was almost always attired casually: in an open neck shirt (check shirts being his favourite); trousers held up with braces; and wearing a fleece in cold weather.

Rebecca referred to her father affectionately as 'Pop'. Her interviews with Miller, and film clips of him and others, were set against various backdrops: Miller relaxing in the garden and reading *The New York Times* while Rebecca sketched, and painted with oil paints and easel; Miller strolling across the lawn with his two German shepherd dogs, or stocking his pond with fish. In some of the film clips, Rebecca is interviewing her father when he is at work in his capacious and well-equipped workshop.[1]

As a playwright Miller was concerned with serious subjects such as social marginalisation, victimisation, injustice, etc. However, in everyday life, with his wonderfully expressive face, a ghost of a smile playing about his lips, or sometimes looking deadpan as he delivered the punch line, he could be humorous and witty.

In Rebecca's film, Miller is seen informing his brother Kermit that when he was drafted into the US Army during the Second World War he was told by the military, 'We don't need you.' The knee, which he had previously damaged playing football, required an operation. 'Why don't you do the op?' Miller enquired. 'They said, "Because it's too dangerous".' The incongruity of this was not lost on Miller, nor was it lost on Kermit, as they sat together roaring with laughter![2]

In the film, Miller described how, twenty-five years previously, he had visited a restaurant, long frequented by his family, where the waiter had leant over the table and told him, 'Your father was a better dresser!'. Miller chuckled at this recollection, demonstrating not only his keen sense of humour but also the fact that he could take a joke against himself.[3]

Miller told the story of how a friend once introduced him to a lady who enquired, 'What is he?' Meaning his religion. The friend replied, 'Hebrew' – i.e. Jewish. To which the lady replied firmly, in reference to the Jews, 'Well, as long as they believe in Christ!' Again, Miller found this encounter highly amusing.[4]

Delightful and endearing film clips exist of Miller swinging his daughter Jane, as a small child, round and round by an arm and a leg; steadying her as a toddler when she was attempting her first steps and making sure she did not fall over; pushing her along on her bicycle; cradling his son Bobby in his arms; showing Rebecca her birthday cake as she pretends to feed her toy poodle; and finally lying on the ground beside a swinging hammock which contained both Inge and Rebecca.[5]

Said Rebecca of her father:

> He would confide in me. He would talk to me about his worries, about being able to write. I don't know if I answered a lot of the time. But the father that I knew, for the most part was very funny, cuddly, jokey. We could laugh so much.

While Miller was wrapping a bread loaf that he had baked, prior to putting it in the freezer, Rebecca asked him, 'Dad, what does this remind you of?' To this, he replied, 'It reminds me of wrapping a cake for my mother, except we didn't have a freezer, and we didn't have a cake.' Here again, Miller reveals his wonderful sense of humour, while at the same time hinting at previously experienced hard times. At one point in the film, Miller is enjoying his woodwork and happy and content in the presence of his daughter, he breaks into a joyful song: 'I'm going to sit right down and write myself a letter, And make believe it came from you.'[6]

Latterly, daughters Jane and Rebecca are seen with their father in his workshop: Miller sitting in a chair with a towel round his neck, while Rebecca cuts his hair with comb and scissors to his instructions. 'The object is to cut them [the hairs] all even, so I don't look like funny!' said Miller, before yelling out when she accidentally nicks him with the self-same scissors.[7]

In the film, Inge appeared, walking down a path through the woods that Miller had made specially. Said she, 'Tomorrow, we should take another walk up in the woods, with a hard-boiled egg' – i.e. on a picnic. To this, Miller replied with characteristic humour, 'Yes, we can plant a hard-boiled egg in the woods.'[8]

Chapter 22

Daniel Miller

Miller and Inge's second child, Daniel, was born in a New York City hospital on 7 January 1967. When Inge gave birth to a son, Bob recalled: 'Dad called and said it was a Down syndrome baby, that the baby was a boy, and that he and Inge were deciding what to do.'

Down (formerly 'Down's) Syndrome was first described in 1862, by UK physician John Langdon Down (1828–1896). The disorder causes intellectual impairment and physical abnormalities.[1]

When Bob asked his father to explain what he meant, Miller replied, 'We may decide that he'll be better off in an institution.' This is what the doctors had advised. According to Inge, mothers of children born with Down syndrome were told by the doctors 'not to bring the children home', and that it was better 'for them to grow up in a different environment'.[2]

Within days Daniel was placed in an institution for infants in New York. At the age of 4 he was admitted to Southbury Training School, an institution for the 'mentally retarded' in Connecticut, situated a short motor car drive from the Millers' home at Roxbury. When Daniel was in his late teens he was released from Southbury and went to live in a 'group home', with five housemates.

Suzanne Andrews, contributing editor at *Vanity Fair*, gave the following account of Daniel's life. By the mid-1990s she said:

> Daniel was doing so well that he was enrolled in a state-financed 'Supported-Living Program' that enabled him to stay in an apartment with a room-mate. He still had

someone looking in on him once a day; helping him to pay bills and sometimes to cook, but otherwise he was on his own. He had a bank account and a job: first at a local gym, and then at a supermarket. He went to parties and concerts, and he loved to go out dancing. He was also a 'natural athlete', said one social worker. He learned to ski, and competed in the Special Olympics in that sport, as well as in cycling, track, and bowling.

Said Richard Godbout, a social worker who had known Daniel for a decade and who ran the Supported Living Program: 'Everyone loved Danny. His greatest joy was helping people. He would insist. If someone needed help moving, Danny was always the first guy to volunteer to help.' Daniel also joined 'Starlight', a national children's charity; and 'People First', a provider of advocacy and representation for those with learning, mental health, of physical disability. He 'wouldn't miss a meeting'.

In September 1995, Daniel, who was then aged 28, met his father for the first time in public, at a conference in Hartford, Connecticut where Miller had come to deliver a speech:

Daniel was there with a large group from 'People First'. Miller, several participants recall, seemed stunned when Danny ran over and embraced him, but recovered quickly. 'He gave Danny a big hug,' says one man. 'He was very nice.' They had their picture taken together, and then Miller left. 'Danny was thrilled', Bowen [Daniel's social worker] recalls.

According to Francine du Plessix Gray, French-born US writer and literary critic, Rebecca's husband Daniel Day-Lewis 'was the most compassionate about Daniel. He always visited him with Inge and Rebecca. Inge told me that she went to see him almost every Sunday, and that [Arthur] never wanted to see him.'

In the late 1990s, Miller made his first and only appearance:

'at one of Daniel's annual "overall plan of service" reviews. The meeting was held in Daniel's apartment and lasted about two hours, Godbout recalls. As Arthur and Inge listened, the social workers who worked with Daniel discussed his progress: his job, his self-advocacy work, his huge network of friends. Miller "was just blown away", Godbout recalled. "He was absolutely amazed at Danny being able to live out on his own. He said it, over and over again: 'I would never have dreamed this for my son. If you would have told me when he first started out that he would get to this point, I would never have believed it'. And you could see his sense of pride. Danny was right there, and he was just beaming".' From then on, 'every now and then a social worker would drive Daniel to New York City to see his parents'.

When Miller's sister Joan, who had never met Daniel, asked her brother, 'Does he know you?' Miller replied, 'Well, he knows I'm a person, and he knows my name, but he doesn't understand what it means to be a son'.

As for Daniel, according to one of his social workers, he:

> did not really think of Arthur and Inge as his parents. The people who played that role in his life were an older couple who had met Daniel after his discharge from Southbury. 'They were the ones you called when Danny needed anything. Money, anything – and you'd get it. We always assumed it came from the Millers, but they weren't the ones you talked to.'

Suzanne Andrews:

> Daniel spent holidays with the couple. Inge would visit, sometimes with Rebecca, and then return home to Roxbury to celebrate with friends and the rest of the Miller

116

family. On Christmas of 2001, after years of noticing that Inge would disappear for several hours on weekends, Copeland [Joan] finally asked where she was going. 'To see Danny,' Inge said. 'Would you like to come?' I said, 'Oh, yes, I would *love* to.' So, I did see him, and I was very very impressed.

Under the terms of a trust created by Miller, Daniel was to receive a share of his estate equal to that of his other three children: Rebecca, Rebecca's half-sister Jane, and her half-brother Bob.

Writing in the year 2007, two years after Miller's death, Suzanne Andrews stated:

> Today, Daniel Miller lives with the elderly couple who have long taken care of him, in a sprawling addition to their home that was built especially for him. He continues to receive daily visits from a state social worker, whom he's known for years. Although his father left him enough money to provide for everything he needs, Daniel has kept his job, which he loves.

Furthermore, said Suzanne, according to Rebecca, Daniel was 'very proud' of his job. As for Rebecca herself, she 'visits him with her family on holidays and during the summers. Danny, said Rebecca, 'is very much part of our family,' and he 'leads a very active, happy life, surrounded by people who love him.[3]

Those who criticise Miller for not caring for Daniel at home, and for meeting with him only infrequently during his lifetime, ignore the fact that the climate was different in the 1960s from what it is today. According to the National Association for Down Syndrome (NADS):

> During the first half of the twentieth century in the United States, the majority of children with Down syndrome were

placed in institutions – frequently soon after birth. This resulted in great human sacrifice for those individuals and for their families, who were convinced, often by members of the medical community, that the child was less than human and that their needs would be so great, their families would not be able to raise them. These children were 'warehoused' in large, state institutions – often in deplorable conditions.

All this would change, however, thanks to the formation of the National Association for Down Syndrome (NADS), 'founded in Chicago in 1960 by Kay McGee, shortly after her daughter, Tricia was born with Down syndrome.' Standard advice back then was for 'parents to institutionalise their newborn infants with Down syndrome. Parents who did not follow this advice took their babies home without support or services. Kay and [her husband] Marty McGee chose to ignore the advice of their paediatrician and they took Tricia home.'

When Daniel was born in January 1967, NADS (then still known as the 'Mongoloid Development Council', or MDC) was in its infancy. Had Daniel been born a decade later, he and his family would have offered such support, and the outcome might have been very different. Had Daniel been raised at home by a loving father and mother, then Miller would in all probability have bonded with the child and thus been a real father to him.

Miller himself elaborated on the dilemma that he had faced when, in his *Journal* in 1968, he wrote as follows:

> As the nurse was dressing Daniel in the hospital, preparing him for our journey to the institution, I turned to examine him – with some difficulty. In a few seconds, I found myself, not doubting the doctor's conclusions, but feeling a welling up of love for him. I dared not touch him, lest I end up by taking him home, and I wept.'

118

Daniel was 50 when Rebecca's film, *Arthur Miller: Writer* was released on 8 December 2017, and she explained:

> The reason I'm not showing my brother in this film is to protect his privacy, but he does have a very happy life now, and an independent life, and we've become very close. My mother visited my brother all his life, but she was somewhat isolated in that. [However] Over the years, my father visited him more and more and he developed more and more of a relationship with him. But publicly, he never mentioned him, and he wasn't in the autobiography. It wasn't easy for either of my parents to talk about him.

Rebecca reflected on her dilemma over whether to include Daniel in her film:

> I had the opportunity to finish this film in the 1990s, but I didn't know how to finish the film without talking about my brother, and I didn't really know how to do that. And I told my father this and he offered to do an interview about it. And I put it off. I put it off for a long time, and I had children, and I started making other films, and he [Miller] died and now we will never know what that interview would have said.[4]

It is likely that both Rebecca and her father were concerned about the impact on Daniel of the publicity he would have received, had he been included in the film.

Chapter 23

Miller's Disillusionment with Marxism/Communism: Religion and the Afterlife

Karl Marx and Friedrich Engels predicted the revolutionary overthrow of capitalism by the proletariat and the eventual attainment of a classless communist society,[1] communism being defined as:

> a theory or system of social organisation in which all property is owned by the community and each person contributes and receives according to their ability and needs; a theory or system of this kind derived from Marxism and established in the former Soviet Union, China, and elsewhere.[2]

According to Rebecca, 'Daddy had been radicalised by Marxism when he was in his teens, but soon came to feel that there wasn't enough room for the individual in Marxism.'[3] And Miller cherished above all, his absolute right to express his views in his plays.

In 1999, Kermit told Miller that in the 1930s, he himself had been a member of the Communist Party. 'It was a point of view,' he declared, 'and lots of people were involved in that kind of thing.'[4]

In 2003, Miller revealed how, in March 1949 at the Waldorf Conference, he had:

> felt uncomfortable, to tell you the truth, because ...
> I was not prepared to dump these people [the Russian

120

people] who I thought had saved Europe, and probably the Jewish population of Europe. Without them I think there would have been a deal between Britain and the Germans. They would have had to have a deal, and the United States would've gone along, and there would have been support here for it, too. I couldn't forget all that. It was impossible. So I was caught in the middle. At the same time some of the left/communist positions made me very, very unhappy.[5]

Miller was certainly not blind to the injustices of communism. Said he, in his autobiography: 'No one needs to convince me that there are certain injustices and excesses which can be laid to the Soviet Union.'[6] More than once, he referred to Marxism in the past tense. For example: 'From such Marxism as I had once espoused, I had not wanted anything for myself, that was certain; it had been far less a political than a moral act of solidarity with all those who had failed in life ....'[7]

Again, writing in the past tense, Miller declared:

I had indeed at times believed with passionate moral certainty, that in Marxism was the hope of mankind and of the survival of reason itself, only to come up against nagging demonstrations of human perversity, not least my own. In the plays and novels about the heroism of the Spanish Civil War and then, now long-forgotten German resistance to Hitlerism − in the whole left-wing liturgy − to be Red [communist or socialist] was to embrace hope, the hope that lies in action. So it had seemed for a time. But I have come to see an altogether different reality after travelling in the Soviet Union, particularly, and in Eastern Europe and China.

What distressed Miller most was to see how, under communism, people became simply pawns, robots, whose every thought, every decision, and every action was dictated by the Party: 'Deep within Marxism, ironically enough, lies a despairing passivity before History, and indeed power is forbidden for the individual and rightfully belongs only to the collective [i.e. state-controlled farms and industries].'

Not for nothing did Miller choose to call his autobiography 'Timebends', for he realised that with the passage of time, events can assume a different reality: 'History bends; the ease with which I could, in the sixties, understand the fear and frustration of the dissident in the Sovietized world was the result, in some great part, of my experience before the Un-American Activities Committee in the fifties.'[8] In other words, the HUAC had behaved precisely like the Soviet government in its attempt to stifle freedom of speech.

In October 1986, Mikhail Gorbachev, General Secretary of the Communist Party of the Soviet Union, invited Miller to meet him. Whereupon Miller took the opportunity tell Gorbachev that whereas 'Marx ruled Russia, and [economist and philosopher] Adam Smith [ruled] the American administration,' the outcome was a 'computerised, televised, half-starved and half-luxuriating world' in the Soviet Union, 'a world with a shrinking proletariat and a burgeoning middle class (despite Marx)', and in the USA and other capitalist countries, a 'growing mass of the starving or the merely hungry and deranged wandering the cities … (despite Adam Smith)'. In other words, ideology – both capitalism and communism, was the root of the problem.

What of religion, and the possibility of an afterlife?

On the subject of religion, Miller was interviewed in 2003 by British theatre and opera director, actor, author and television presenter, Jonathan Miller (1934–2019). Whereupon the interviewer was absolutely delighted to have discovered in his namesake Miller, another atheist!

During his childhood in Brooklyn, said [Arthur] Miller, his family practised the Jewish religion, but only to the extent of:

> observing two or three times a year. Apart from that they were busy trying to make a living. If they were anything, they were observant or orthodox, but that only occurred during high holidays. The rest of the time they were free to do whatever they wanted. They didn't go to the synagogue every Saturday. They didn't pray. It was kind of an obedient nod in the right direction.
>
> I tried to be a religious person when I was 12, 13, 14. It lasted about two years, and then it simply vanished. I simply laid down one evening to go to sleep and I woke up the next day and it wasn't there anymore. And I guess it was part of my growing up that I would be searching for my roots somewhere, and I found them elsewhere. I didn't find them in religion. In my late teens I began reading and surmising that the idea of religion was a creation of man's longing to signify, to be a permanent part of the universe.

Miller's doubts were reinforced by the economic downturn in the USA known as the 'Great Depression': 'Religion, especially in the Depression of the '30s, seemed absolutely absurdly irrelevant. We were in the midst of a terrific social crisis here, and the religious, in general, had nothing to say about it.'

'Oh God! It's exhausting to know where to begin, to throw light on this whole thing … Christian zealots believe that Christ will return when the Jews become Christians. This news is gonna come as a shock to most of the Jews when they hear it! But that's the program. That Armageddon comes, at which point the Jews become believers in Christ, and Christ returns, and we are off to the races.'[9]

In fact, in Judaism, Christ is considered to be neither a prophet nor the messiah, nor the son of God.

Miller summed up the position as follows:

> Philosophically, if I can use that word, it just seems to
> me so patent that what man has done is to project himself
> into the heavens where he can be all powerful, as he's
> not here, and moral, and decent, and vengeful, and all the
> things he's not allowed to do on the earth, and to don that
> white garment and the beard, and to be what he wished in
> his dreams he could be. And I can't get past that.[10]

In other words, 'God', 'Heaven', and religion itself were simply
constructs of the human mind. Jonathan Miller certainly concurred
with such sentiments.

Despite being an acknowledged atheist, did Miller believe in a life
after death? asked Jonathan Miller:

> Everything I say, which is very sceptical, if not worse,
> is conditioned by one thing, and that is, we don't know
> where life started, or how. Nobody really knows that. And
> death, the end of consciousness, is the awesome mystery
> that anybody who has lived through it all [presumably
> by being in the presence of death] knows that he has no
> answer to it.

Miller declared that he 'could no longer contain the idea', that life
continued in some disembodied form. And yet for him, hope sprung
eternal. 'The idea that that consciousness could vanish, be no more,
is unacceptable,' he said. 'I have no way of accepting this.' As for
the possibility of life after death, 'That's what I find myself hoping.'
It was his opinion that, even after death, consciousness 'does continue
in art. The artist finally leaves us with his consciousness.'

Miller's wife Inge had died on 30 January 2002, and eighteen
months later, he had not disposed of her possessions. 'I'm surrounded

by all her stuff, of her life, and the idea that she's not here defeats some impulse to recreate her, but I know that the impulse is simply the inability to accept this absurdity, that all that consciousness and all that beauty simply isn't there anymore.'

Did Miller have any expectation of a 'rendezvous' with Inge at some time in the future? 'No, this is beyond me,' he said. 'I don't have that at all. I don't believe.' Only memory remained. If there *was* a consciousness which outlasted the death of the body, he continued, 'it would be lovely. But, of course,' he said with typical humour, 'there would be so many of us. It would be a rather crowded area. I think it would be like the subway at 5.00 o'clock in the evening. You would wish you could get off, I think.'

Nonetheless, Miller admitted, 'the urge' was 'always there … and if you're not careful, I suppose you could venture into [believing in] everlasting life'. Miller had confronted the terrible dilemma which all human beings have to confront, at some stage, namely the impossibility of believing that death and the consequent separation from loved ones, is the end.[11]

Chapter 24

Anti-Semitism: The Danger of Religion Wedded to Nationalism

In his discussion with Jonathan Miller, Arthur Miller now addressed the subject of anti-Semitism. One reason for anti-Semitism said Miller, is that because a Jew does not believe in Jesus Christ, he or she is therefore perceived as being an atheist. Or 'if not an atheist, then pretty close,' Miller continued. 'A heathen, perhaps.'[1]

Despite being a self-proclaimed atheist, this did not prevent Miller from realising that lessons can be learned from religion.

His play, *The Creation of the World and Other Business*, he said, was about *Genesis,* the first book of the Bible, which includes an account of the creation of the world:[2]

> I didn't mean to, but I got involved with the Bible in the way that I never had before. It's very interesting that the old rabbis, or whoever put the Bible together, which was obviously written by different people at different times in history, they could have chosen any book to start the Bible ... and they opened with a fratricide.

This is a reference to the story of Cain and his younger brother Abel, sons of Adam and Eve. Both brothers made offerings to God, who favoured Abel's offering above that of Cain. Whereupon Cain murdered Abel. Both brothers were Jewish.

126

Anti-Semitism became superimposed on the story when, as Miller pointed out, in order to place Abel in a better light, he was subsequently portrayed as a Gentile, whereas Cain remained the 'villainous Jew'. Miller went on to discuss how a given group of people may demonise another group, using religion as its pretext.

> I suppose it's inevitable, and always will be there to some degree, that one's own group, being most familiar, is less dangerous than an out-group, which is always menacing because it's strange. They look different. They don't speak the way we do. They break their boiled egg at the narrow end instead of the broad end. This is going to go on for ever. But when politicians seize upon these differences, or these apprehensions, and when they make religious differences the centre of the political program, that's when the end is nigh.

Jonathan Miller asked Miller if to be an atheist in the USA was regarded as subversive, politically incorrect, and unacceptable. Whereupon Miller agreed that there was now a tendency for politicians to equate belief in the Christian religion with patriotism:

> Certainly, the religious overlay of patriotism has come into fashion. It's always there, of course, in this country. We've more people go to church here than I think anywhere. But it's gotten heavier now. They invoke God at any opportunity, whether its buying an automobile or [whatever], because it's such an easy way to cuddle up to what they think the majority is about, which is this slavish kind of worship of something. It's a political event.

In former times, said Miller, he could not recall the government: 'calling upon faith-based agencies to take care of the sick, and the unemployed, and the rest of it'. Formerly, 'the government simply did these things'.

Did the enterprise in Iraq have a faith-based, Christian patriotism? This was a reference to the Iraq War (20 March 2003 to 15 December 2011). Again, Miller agreed: 'I suppose that we did that in the Second World War, to a degree, but it was never laid on with a trowel this way. I think Roosevelt called upon God occasionally, but it didn't bother him too much.'

But Roosevelt:

> was not using it. This is now being used as a means of persuasion. It's patent. It's obvious. They call upon God to initiate a program, whatever it may be, a civil program of some sort. And they lard it over with some religious verbiage, make it seem as though if you oppose this, you oppose the Lord.
>
> There are a lot of Americans, I think they're a minority but they're very vocal, who are really aching for an ayatollah [a high-ranking religious leader among the Shiite Muslims, especially in Iran[3]].
>
> I think they would love to have a department of religion, and go back to the early seventeenth century perhaps, and have an official church. But they have convinced a lot of people to forget that this country was founded by people who were really escaping the domination of a governmental religion, and who breathed freely here with gratitude that they didn't have to obey a churchly government.

For Miller, that religion should dominate and decide the politics of a nation was an absolute anathema. Such an eventuality, he declared forcibly, was 'something that has to be resisted on principle from one generation to another. At the moment, it's tougher than ever because the government itself is blatantly on the side of an official religion, I think.'

The 'real issue' that was 'bothering him' said Miller, was the attempt by the 'so-called religious', whom he considered to be 'nationalist people', rather than religious, to wed Christianity or Judaism with nationalism. This, in his opinion was 'lethal'. Miller gave vent to his feelings concerning the dangers of religion:

> I suppose every violent conflict in the world now is being led by priests, rabbis, or Muslim clerics. It's really quite amazing. I wonder whether it's ever happened in hundreds and hundreds of years? It's the church militant, in all these religions. They've moved in. They've added that lethal mixture of religion and nationalism to the programmes that they sell, and the reason it's lethal is because to believe in a religion means that you don't believe in a different religion. You can't believe in two religions. You can believe in one, and the other ones are wrong and deserve to be combated and destroyed. I mean, it's implicit in the whole idea of religious belief, I think, in the normal way that religious belief is thought of. You can't be both a Catholic and a Protestant.[4]

In other words, religion is an inherently divisive phenomenon.

Chapter 25

Miller: an Abhorrence of Racism

Miller's biographer, Christopher Bigsby, cited several examples of Miller's abhorrence of racism. For example, during his childhood in Harlem:

> my school had a lot of black kids in it, although most of them didn't stay. They just disappeared. I can't say I was ever a friend of theirs because they hung [out] together, but they were always, to me, figures of great anguish. I always felt badly about them. I had a very instantaneous feeling of identification with them. I felt close to them.
>
> We lived on 110 Street. By the time you got to 116 Street there were a number of black families and I used to ride my bike through there a lot, and they were always very nice to me.[1]

During his first year at the University of Michigan, 1934/35, the visiting Georgia Tech football team refused to play the home team, the Michigan Wolverines, on the grounds that it included an African-American, Willis Franklin Ward. Ward was also an outstanding track and field athlete, who had outsprinted Jessie Owens (who went on to win four gold medals in the 1936 Olympic Games) on more than one occasion. When Miller protested, the visiting team members 'told him that they would actually kill Ward if he set foot on the Michigan gridiron [field on which American Football is played].' Whereupon Miller wrote an article of protest to the *Michigan Daily* newspaper, 'but it was not published'.[2]

In October 1941 Miller intervened, unsuccessfully, with the head of a new shipyard constructed by Black workers at Cape Fear,

Wilmington, North Carolina. This was because, having constructed the shipyard, the Black workforce were then laid off. Couldn't they have been hired as labour in the building of the ships also, Miller enquired? 'Oh, no. The Whites wouldn't work with them,' came the reply. Miller described this as 'Such an overt act of discrimination that it was breathtaking. It was fierce. It was total.'[3]

In an interview with Stephen R. Centola, Assistant Professor of English at Virginia Polytechnic Institute and State University in 1984, Miller proposed a possible solution to the problem of Black versus White racism. 'I regard racism as a class phenomenon,' he declared. 'I was born in Harlem, and I saw it happen in Harlem.' The reason why Black people were not 'acceptable', he continued, was 'more for the fact that they are working-class or poor, than because they are black. If in a short period of time, by some miracle, they were hundreds and hundreds of thousands of black professionals, middle-class people, the thing would begin to fade.' Miller compared the situation of Black people with that of the Arab people. Formerly, 'a creature of ridicule,' he said, 'the Arab', once they became wealthy, achieved 'a new class identity', and 'took on a new kind of persona, a new kind of dignity'.[4]

Miller's (unpublished) novel *The Bangkok Star* was inspired by a sea voyage that he made to the Gulf of Mexico. In the novel, two men of African-American descent are sent to join the crew of the ship *Calhoun*, which is crewed by white men from the southern US state of Alabama. Miller deliberately named his fictitious ship after John Caldwell Calhoun (1782 to 1850), vice president of the USA from 1825 to 1832, and a strong defender of slavery. In the novel, the black crewmembers are ill-treated and racially abused.

The Bangkok Star, said Bigsby, was 'as direct a denunciation of racism' as is to be found 'in the work of any white American author outside of Faulkner or James T. Farrell'. This was a reference to US writer and Nobel laureate William Faulkner (1897-1962) from Oxford, Mississippi; and to US novelist, short-story writer, and poet James Thomas Farrell (1904 to 1979) from Chicago, Illinois.

Chapter 26

1992: The State of the Theatre

In 1992 Miller, aged 76, was interviewed by Charlie Rose about the current state of the theatre which was a subject very close to his heart. After all this was not only his livelihood, it was also the way in which he got his message across.

The interview could have been handled better. Rose asked cringeworthy questions along the lines of 'Are you as good now as you once were?'; 'Don't be embarrassed if I mention you in the same breath as Shakespeare', etc. Furthermore, Rose continually attempted to put words in Miller's mouth, and constantly hijacked the conversation by introducing irrelevancies and distractions. Nevertheless, the great playwright responded with patience and courtesy.

The theatre was Miller's passion and also his livelihood. Did he think it was in good health? After all there was talk of a current revival on Broadway. Miller was not optimistic.

> Well, er, count the plays. There aren't many. It's not a revival.
> It's that there are a few musicals that are making a lot of
> money. But the sickness is there, and I don't see any sign of
> it going away. It's simply that they opened a couple of hits
> which were drawn from the past. They're not new shows.[1]

Miller referred to *Crazy for You*, the romantic musical comedy by George and Ira Gershwin by way of example. It opened at the Shubert Theatre on Broadway in 1992, but was largely a reworking of the original 1930 Gershwin musical, *Girl Crazy*.

132

Market forces

According to Miller, the problem in regard to theatre was the lack of tradition found in the UK.

> what we have now is the ultimate development of the market economy, as far as the theatre is concerned. That is to say, a few shows make a lot of money and they leave nothing behind them when they close. By that I mean, we don't have a theatre culture. We don't have a group of actors gradually developing their art over periods of years so that you get an Olivier, you get a Richardson, you get any number of absolutely accomplished actors.
>
> [Instead] We get people who are in and out, and they're in and out not because they're not nice people. It's just that the situation makes it impossible for an actor to remain in the theatre for the most part.[2]

Another problem of fundamental importance was that there was insufficient funding to keep the theatre alive.

Sweden, and the importance of continuity

Miller was, of course, an international phenomenon whose plays were staged all over the world, so he had experience of how the theatre operated in other countries: 'I just directed *Death of a Salesman* in Stockholm. They have a theatre with six stages in it, ninety actors, under 365 days a year contracts.' Many of the actors were experienced and had played a variety of parts, he said.

> Everybody in that cast has a background, that may be only two or three people in this country have. If I want

to build airplanes, I don't go out on 46th Street and ask anybody, 'Do you know how to build an airplane? If so, come in. We'll talk to you.' These people are hired, and they are kept there, and they're embedded in an 'airplane culture'. You see, we don't do that.

Competition from the film industry

Another reason for the decline of the theatre was that actors could earn far more money in the film industry. Miller found it frustrating that you could 'write a wonderful part, and you can't get actors to play it for more than two or three months'. Actors on Broadway were earning a mere 750 dollars a week, whereas 'Any one of those actors working in television or on a film, would work the same amount of time for several hundred thousand dollars, if not more. So, you're asking *them* to support the theatre. So why should they do that?'[3]

'When you try to cast a play here, you've got to go to a handful of movie stars who are still interested in playing the theatre.' And because of their commitments elsewhere, 'these people could only remain for a couple of months in the theatre before going off to make their next film. So, when you say, is there a revival, I tell you nothing has changed.'

Was this the end of an era?

Rose asked whether the era of the great playwrights over. 'I'm not prepared to say that it's over,' said Miller, 'why, someone might be writing a masterpiece at that very moment. However, I could repeat, boringly admit, that the situation in the theatre repels that kind of talent. You see, we blew the audience.' Theatre prices were 'too high', he said, 'so much so that 'a lot of people who would love to go simply cannot go. I mean, schoolteachers, intellectuals, people who don't make a lot of money. It's really insane.'

Despite the success of his play *Death of a Salesman* (1949), said Miller, he and other playwrights felt that they were operating in a hostile environment as far as the media was concerned. He confessed that he had many regrets about his life, one of which was that had he 'been connected with a real theatre', there would have been 'a friendly atmosphere, where people [the management] wanted your stuff, rather than a group of gamblers, really, who were looking at this and saying, "Can we make our money back twice, double, triple?"' And the outcome would have been that 'there would have been twice as many plays. It sounds crazy but I think so'.

Small is beautiful!

Miller went on to explain how British playwright Alan Ayckbourn, Artistic Director at Scarborough Library Theatre, had solved the problem in the UK:

> by establishing a small theatre in the small town where he comes from, about forty to fifty miles away from London. [Scarborough is actually 240 miles from London!] He's got a nice, tidy little audience there, but he writes the kind of a play which is perfectly admirable, [even though] it's not my kind of a play.

It was Ayckbourn who, in 1987, had directed 'that marvellous production of *The View from the Bridge* in London,' said a delighted Miller, 'which was the last thing I would ever have dreamed he would ever do'.[4]

Chapter 27

Miller's Opinion of US Politicians

In assessing the various merits and demerits of the US Presidents and senior politicians who had served during his lifetime, Miller was under no illusions: he knew who had acted as a good and responsible leader with the interests of the American people at heart, and who had not.

In 1992, Charlie Rose asked Miller if the American public was attracted to US businessman, philanthropist and Independent politician Ross Perot, because at present the public felt disenfranchised by the gridlock in Washington and they wanted a leader, someone who could 'fix it'. In that year, Perot stood as Independent presidential candidate against Republican President George H.W. Bush (1924–2018) (41st President, 1989–1993), and William Jefferson ('Bill') Clinton (b. 1946), (Democrat and 42nd President, 1993–2001.)

It was Miller's opinion that the current political gridlock had arisen because of the 'divided party control of the legislature and executive branches of government,' and the fact that 'the policy preferences of the two parties [Republican and Democratic] had been increasingly polarised'.[1] As regards Perot, said Miller, although he did not profess to know all the answers, his byword was, 'there is no problem that we can't solve'. This was leadership, and 'that was what the country needed'. But were people aware of what they were voting for? In respect of Perot, Miller continued: 'the most alarming thing about that whole phenomenon is that you ask people, well why exactly are you backing this man, and they don't know. I mean, what does he stand for that you like?'[2]

When asked which of the various Presidents of the USA during Miller's lifetime was the best, he replied that Roosevelt 'was the matrix that they're all trying to imitate. Roosevelt was the man of our era'. Looking back, Miller described how, when Roosevelt was elected President in 1933, he had been forced to change his policies. Roosevelt 'was a conservative', a 'rich man', who 'came in preaching a balanced budget. He wasn't coming in to spend all this money, on WPA, and welfare, and the rest of it. Far from it.' This was a reference to the Works Progress Administration (WPA), which employed millions of job seekers to carry out public works projects. However, Miller continued, 'within 8–10 months he realised that the whole thing was going down the tubes unless something very different was done, namely to start spending some money, and that violated all the tenets of his original election.' In other words, the sensible politician takes heed of the electorate and adapts to circumstances.

Rose quoted Roosevelt as having said, 'we have nothing to fear but fear itself', to which Miller replied: 'That is leadership. And, by the way, Perot has got a similar kind of attitude, that there is no problem we can't solve.'

What of Adlai Stevenson, who ran (unsuccessfully) against US army general and Republican Dwight D. Eisenhower (1890–1969) (34th President, 1953–1961), in the 1952 US Presidential Election?

> He was about the best of them, but he made terrible speeches. If you look at Stevenson's speeches, read them, they are so prolix [using too many words: tediously lengthy[3]]. The sentence structure is so involved. They aren't good speeches. They're good reading, but the ear wasn't there. And he loved these elliptical statements which read so well but when you try to figure, they were rather Germanic sentences and by the time you got to the end you've forgot what the beginning was.[4]

For Miller the playwright, the power of the spoken word far exceeded that of the written word.

As regards Democrat John F. Kennedy (1917–1963) (35th President, from January 1961 until his assassination on 22 November 1963), Miller declared:

> I've met him a couple of times. I can't say that I knew him. I wasn't mad about him. It took me a little while to vote for him, because I felt that he was a hawk [a person who advocates an aggressive or warlike policy, especially in foreign affairs[5]]. I felt that he was going to get us into a war. I felt he was elitist, and I didn't like the smell of him. He was a little too stylish for me.

According to Miller, Republican and former actor Ronald W. Reagan (1911–2004) (40th President, 1981–1989) was an example of the weak leadership which caused so many problems for the US. He felt that Reagan had been out of touch with the people. 'It's authority that people want … Reagan was a man who wasn't there. Everybody knew he wasn't there, and they sensed he wasn't there.' But, paradoxically, 'That's what they liked about him!' Miller did admit, however, that President Reagan 'had a great feel for the ordinary person'. Also, that he expressed the sentiment of the nation, which was 'the important thing, if you want to be a leader'.

In respect of politicians in general, said an exasperated Miller:

> Well I wish to God that somebody would be talking about the issues, instead of making 'poetic statements' about 'this is what I can do', and 'this is what I'm going to do'. What they should be doing is confronting real issues, like 'how do you start to educate this population so that they can even start to run the machines that you've got?'.

And doubtless, knowing Miller's track record, a politician who concerned him or herself with social justice, fairness, and equality would be a sine qua non!

Chapter 28

Some Other Plays and Writings: *Mr Peters' Connections* (1998)

When Miller left the University of Michigan in 1938, he wrote a tragic play about the conquest of Mexico by Spanish conquistador Hernán Cortés, whose expedition (1519–21) led to the fall of the Aztec Empire, and the fascinating story of Montezuma II (c.1466 – 29 June 1520), ninth ruler of the Aztec Empire. The play revealed Miller's taste for the dramatic.

'The tragedy had about twenty-five characters in it,' he said, 'which was an absurdity as far as getting it produced in the commercial theatre, which regarded an eight-character play as being excessive. So, I couldn't get that produced.' Alternatively, Miller had hoped that the Federal Theatre, which was subsidised by the government, would stage the play, but the theatre 'folded within six or eight months after I got onto it. So, I never did get that play produced at all, excepting many years later in England, where they did it on television and they did many readings of it.'[1] Unfortunately, the life of the creative artist is not without its disappointments!

An article by Miller entitled 'Tragedy and the Common Man' was published in the *New York Times* in 1949. Here, he argued that the 'Common Man' was as appropriate a subject 'for tragedy in its highest sense as kings were'.

I Don't Need You Any More (1959) is a short story by Miller in which a 5-year-old boy is trying to make sense of the world in which he finds himself. Miller: 'we are formed in this world when we are sons and daughters, and the first truths we know throw us into conflict with our fathers and mothers. The struggle for mastery – for the freedom of manhood or womanhood – is the struggle not only to overthrow authority but reconstitute it anew.'[2]

With considerable insight, UK literary analyst and novelist Christopher Bigsby comments that Miller has 'tried to re-inhabit his younger self, to convey some sense of his struggle for autonomy, and to account for the complex feelings towards his parents that have left him with a residue of guilt'.[3]

In 1992, Miller stated that he was currently working on *The Last Yankee*, which went on to premiere at the Manhattan Theatre Club, New York, on 5 January 1993. This was a compassionate play about two women patients, 'Patty' and 'Karen', who were in a psychiatric hospital and suffering from mental health problems. Patty's husband Leroy was a carpenter – and Miller's hobby was carpentry. So, was this play autobiographical? Charlie Rose enquired. To this, Miller replied, 'anybody who writes, writes about what he lives and knows'.[4] It is more than likely his late wife Marilyn, who suffered from mental health problems, was very much in Miller's mind when he wrote this play.

Miller's play, *Broken Glass* premiered at the Long Wharf Theatre, New Haven, Connecticut, in March 1994, and at the Booth Theatre on Broadway on 24 April 1994. Its name derives from the German 'Kristallnacht' (the *Night of Broken Glass*), the occasion of concerted violence by Nazis throughout Germany and Austria against Jews and their property on the night of 9–10 November 1938.[5] *Broken Glass* is the story of Sylvia and Phillip Gellburg, a middle-class Jewish couple living in Brooklyn in 1938. Sylvia becomes mysteriously paralysed, having heard of Nazi violence against Jews in Europe. The subject of the Nazi Holocaust, in which some 6 million of his fellow Jews were murdered, was of course never far from Miller's mind.

Miller's play *Mr Peters' Connections* premiered at the Signature Theatre Company, Manhattan on 28 April 1998. This was an 'Off-

Broadway' theatre: a professional Manhattan theatre venue with capacity for 100–499 people (i.e. smaller than the main Broadway theatres). Three years earlier, in 1995, while still working on *Mr Peters' Connections*, Miller said: 'This is not so much a play, but an exploration of the area between life and death, and it may someday be a play.'[6] Although he declared himself to be an atheist, such conundrums as these were clearly in Miller's thoughts.

In the play, the protagonist, former airline pilot Harry Peters, lives in a twilight world of dreams and memories or, in Miller's words, 'in a space where the living and the dead meet'.[7] As for the concept of a deity, Harry declares ruefully, 'God is precisely what is not there when you need him.' Surely, this is a reflection of Miller's views precisely!

On the film's opening night, Miller was told by US playwright John Guare, who was a member of the audience, 'It's great! It was so bold!' But did Miller believe that 'there is a critic in New York who is going to see that?' (i.e. appreciate the play and its meaning.) The answer was no.

Miller could not conceal his disappointment at the adverse criticism the play attracted; 'Well, what can I say?' The view of the critics was, that 'basically, it was boring'. So, Miller concluded despondently and with one particular critic in mind, 'No insights in that. He saw nothing much in it.'

Nonetheless, Miller responded with typical stoicism and determination: 'We'll have to find another way to penetrate, because this will kill it, for this run.' As for the future he remained optimistic, saying, 'I have no questions about it. It will come back,' and then, with typical humour, 'Art is long, life is short. I forgot the Latin!'[8]

Chapter 29

Finishing the Picture (2004): Later Years

Miller was 62 when he sketched the outline of what was to be his final play, *Finishing the Picture*, in 1977–8. This was fifteen years after the death of Marilyn Monroe (5 August 1962). It premiered at the Goodman Theatre, Chicago, on 21 September 2004. The play is, in fact, a remembrance by Miller of the period filming *The Misfits*, starring Marilyn as 'Roslyn Tabler', including her dysfunctional state, and the problems that this caused.

In the play, 'Philip Ochsner' is the producer of the appropriately named Bedlam Pictures Film Company, and 'Derek Clemson' is the director. 'Kitty', the female star of the film, is a thinly disguised Marilyn; 'Paul', the screenwriter and Kitty's husband, is likewise a thinly disguised Miller; and 'Edna Meyers' is Kitty's secretary.

Ochsner describes Kitty as having 'a big funny stare', and he asks Clemson, 'Is that from the drug?' Whereupon Derek replies, 'Pills, yes, and a bad life [one of hardship].' 'Does anyone have any idea what is exactly wrong with her?' asks Ochsner. 'She is a case of terminal disappointment, with herself, her husband, the movies, the United States, the world,' Clemson replies. 'But why?' says Ochsner. 'It seems to me she's got everything. She must be the envy of 90 per cent of humanity.'

Ochsner states of Kitty that he has 'talked to her analyst in New York City for a few minutes', and that the analyst was in favour of having her admitted to hospital. Says Clemson, 'She has ghosts

142

sitting on her chest; ghosts of things she's done, or been done to her; she can't breathe, can't sleep, can't wake, fleeing the hounds of hell.' Says Edna, 'Now she thinks everything is fake ... herself, most of all. And it's terrible.' The parallels between Marilyn and Kitty are obvious: both were addicted to drugs; both had gross inferiority complexes and a total lack of any feelings of self-worth; and both received psychiatric treatment.

Kitty was seeking 'the right to express her grief' says her husband, Paul. This was the grief about:

> having to pretend that she's the happy, radiant carefree girl she was before she had a thought in her head. There is a kind of monster walking step for step behind her whispering in her ear never to trust any anyone; and the trouble is, he has a point. Everyone wants something from her. She certainly is surrounded with resentment now. I think she's not sure she really exists. So, she stays in bed.

Here is Miller, articulating the fact that Kitty, just like Marilyn, has been exploited by others.

'We're far too angry at each other, the bridge is burned,' Paul concludes. 'We each promised to cure the other of his [and her] life [respectively], but we turned out to be exactly who we were. That's a very large disappointment.'

Says Derek of Kitty: 'She's gone through two of the best [psycho] analysts] in the country and left both of them talking to themselves. She's floating out there somewhere beyond science.' So, despite Miller/Paul's best efforts, they have failed to come to the rescue of Marilyn/Kitty.

Edna tells Paul, 'Kitty loves you.' To this, he replies, 'But she doesn't *like* me, Edna. And how could she – I didn't save her. I didn't do the miracle I kind of promised. And she didn't save me, as she promised. I'm afraid of her now – I have no idea what she's going to do next.'

Here is Miller admitting, that just as Marilyn had problems, so also did he. After all, the stress of the situation that Miller found himself in with Marilyn must have taken a great toll on his own mental health. The fictional character 'Kitty' did 'finish the picture', though it is left in the air as to whether or not she survived. As we know, the real life Marilyn tragically did not survive.

Finishing the Picture, is revealing in many ways. Sixteen years after Marilyn's death, he still blamed himself for not succeeding in saving her from suicide. And he continued to attribute her death to the adverse circumstances of her life, and blamed those around her, himself included, for driving her to it.

A question arises: did Marilyn's doctors and analysts make the correct diagnosis of her condition? Hyman Engelberg, her general physician, diagnosed her as 'Manic Depressive, which is now called Bipolar Personality Disorder'; Anna Freud, her psychoanalyst, said she was 'Paranoid with Schizophrenic elements'.[1] Finally, Marilyn's psychiatrist and psychoanalyst, Ralph Greenson, diagnosed Marilyn as a 'Schizophrenic', 'Sick, Borderline, Paranoid Addict'. By 'Borderline', Greenson undoubtedly meant 'Borderline Personality Disorder' – BPD, which was almost undoubtedly the correct diagnosis. (The term 'Borderline Personality' was first proposed by US psychoanalyst Adolph Stern in 1938.)

The next question is, when Miller was married to Marilyn, did Dr Greenson appraise him of the true situation, i.e. that in the main, her BPD was responsible for her mindset and behaviour? If so, this may well have been of some comfort to Miller, in that it would provide an explanation to him of why he was unable to help her. Or did the protocol of medical confidentiality prevent Greenson from so doing? From Miller's own statements, made both by himself and uttered vicariously in his plays, he appears not to have been aware that Marilyn was suffering from BPD.

Had it been otherwise, Marilyn's condition would have been placed in its proper context, and Miller might have been spared the guilt which gnawed away at him for the rest of his life. For Marilyn's condition was so entrenched and intractable, it is likely that there was nothing *anyone* could have done to save her.

What of Miller's later years? In his autobiography *Timebends*, published on 1 November 1987 when Miller was aged 72, he wrote:

> I have lived more than half my life in the Connecticut
> countryside; all the time expecting to get some play
> or book finished, so I can spend more time in the city
> where everything is happening. Little happens here that
> I don't make happen, except the sun coming up and going
> down, and the leaves emerging and dropping off, and an
> occasional surprise like the recent appearance of coyotes
> in the woods.

The truth was, he said, 'that we are all connected, watching one another. Even the trees'.[2] Miller certainly felt in communion with nature.

Meanwhile, Inge was diagnosed with lymphoma. Said Rebecca: 'She lived with it for a couple of years, and Arthur was very close by her, but then suddenly she got very sick and died.' That was on 30 January 2002. 'That came as a shock to him, and he was quite lost after that.'

In May 2002, Miller said: 'I am very old now. Like a dog, I always laid my catch at her [Inge's] feet. Now I carry it around aimlessly, the happy game disrupted, forever.'[3] In that year of 2002, minimalist painter Agnes Barley came to live with Miller at his home in Roxbury, Connecticut.

Chapter 30

Arthur Miller the Playwright

Miller comes across as a quiet, calm, and unflappable individual, yet his plays are highly charged with emotion. They are not for the fainthearted!

Why did Miller choose to become a playwright? asked Charlie Rose.

> Well, it's an affliction that I often think you're born with. I never thought about becoming a playwright or not becoming one. It just seemed to be natural. I think a playwright is partly an actor, frankly. I didn't used to think that, but I think so now, and you are projecting your acting skills on other characters.

For Miller, playwriting was an auditory skill rather than a literary one. The difference between a novelist and an actor, he said, was:

> that usually the novelist is not an actor, so he doesn't hear language, whereas a playwright hears language. You've got to hear what you're writing. I think characters are projections of the author, obviously, and the different sides of his apprehension of reality. If I can't hear it, I can't write it.

When asked what the great playwrights had in common, Miller was unequivocal: 'A fierce moral sensibility, which is unquenchable, and that they are all burning with some anger at the way the world is. The little ones have made a peace with it, and the bigger ones cannot make any peace.'[1]

In respect of his plays, Miller said: 'The big job is not to make simple things complicated, but to make complicated things comprehensible. In other words, I'm the guy that goes around and says, "Well, what is really going on here?"'[2] This was a theme to which Miller constantly returned: the search for the truth.

Asked what he would liked to have been, if not a writer, he said: 'I would have loved to own a farm. But I would not want to do it in an area where you have to clear a lot of rocks out of the way, which is what I had,' referring to his home and estate at Roxbury, Connecticut. 'I love the land. There's a lot of wonderful, interesting work in breeding plants and all that.' Miller pointed out that Thomas J. Jefferson (1743–1826), US statesman and Founding Father, was himself a farmer. However, people who work the land 'have to be more or less able to do all kinds of other techniques, like welding. They have to know about metals. They have to know about wood, weather, soil, a thousand things to do with the machinery.' Judging by film taken of Miller on his Roxbury estate, this was the great playwright to a tee!

In respect of writing in his advancing years, Miller was sanguine: 'The skill is there. It's just that as you grow older, of course, you have to fend off the realisation that this is not going to change the world, which was the illusion you started with.'[3]

Rebecca informed her father that when she was growing up in the 1970s she gained the impression that he 'had a lot of disappointments in the theatre during that time'. To this, he replied, 'Mostly, I would say I agree with you.' She asked whether he ever felt he was losing his muse. to which her father answered: 'I felt that I was out of place, more than anything else. I'll tell you why, concretely, because in Europe my stuff was always accepted. It worked, whether it was in Britain, or Germany, very often France, Italy.'

US playwright and author Tony Kushner described as 'Horrifying, the way Arthur was treated by the critics' who, in his opinion, 'should certainly feel that this is a permanent mark of shame. Just dismissing play, after play, after play. It was a kind of laziness. [As if to say] "Why do we care about what this old man has to say about anything?"'

Said Rebecca, 'I think it was hurtful to him that in his own country, he was dismissed.' But, of course, this was at the dawn of a new era, where the young were interested in popular music, drug taking, and free love. 'But he also had this kind of ebullience and belief in himself,' she continued, 'that just kept bubbling up. That was his essential life force.'

Miller's son Bob described his father's rigorous routine. Despite everything, at '8 o'clock he was at his desk, and he would come down at noon. It was like punching a time clock. He had a working man's schedule. Like a blue-collar ethic of his.' But Miller's creativity was not confined to his playwriting.

Rebecca: 'His idea was that if you could make it yourself you should make it yourself.' For example, he made a coffee table, dining table and bookshelves. Rebecca recalled having asked for a stereo when she was 14 years old, whereupon: 'instead of getting the stereo made of plastic that I was hoping for, that everyone else had, my father made me a stereo out of wood, [having] found these enormous knobs from the dump.'

British journalist and theatre critic Benedict Nightingale was extremely complimentary about Miller's plays, declaring that they had 'a lot to tell us about our time. For example, his play *The American Clock*, which premiered at the Spoleto Festival, Charleston, South Carolina in May 1980 and on Broadway at the Biltmore Theatre on 11 November 1980, 'tells us an awful lot about the Depression, which is something which was definitely formative in his family's life.' This was relevant to the 'economic doldrums of the present time'.[4]

As for *All My Sons* (1947), this 'is about petty swindling, telling lies, and the resultant deaths'. This was relevant 'to what was probably going on in certain "big industries" today.'[5] It was interesting, Nightingale continued, that Miller saw himself 'almost entirely as a theatre writer. He said he thought that a group of people coming together, and perhaps losing themselves collectively in a theatrical experience, was really what mattered, was what he cared about.'[6]

The theme of many of Miller's plays was a person's failure to face up to the truth of his or her situation. Why could they not do so? asked UK broadcaster Melvyn Bragg.

> Because too much has been compromised already. You know, there is an investment. People make an investment in falsehood, invest a whole lifetime in it. And it's not an inability to see the truth. It's an inability to start over again, and an age comes when it's impossible, it can't be done. So, what you try to do is to prove the unprovable, and continue on to the grave, to reinforce it and to justify it, because to overturn it is too painful or too expensive.[7]

Here, *Death of a Salesman* comes to mind, in which the fictional character 'Willy Loman', like millions of others in real life, persists in attempting, unsuccessfully, to realise for himself 'The American Dream'.

Rebecca believed that US actor and film-maker Dustin Hoffman's revival of *Death of a Salesman* (in 1985) 'was the beginning of a kind of renaissance. 'All the plays started to get done again in this country, and all over the world.' As for Miller, 'It was the happiest thing of my professional life, I think,' he said. 'I mean, some of these plays are fifty years old. There aren't many things in this culture that are fifty years old and are still usable.' This time the criticisms were favourable, demonstrating just how fickle critics can be. 'Well, you see if you wait long enough,' said Miller philosophically.

Miller told Rebecca that the film of his play *The Crucible* (1996)

> is going to start shooting in about a week. My son, Bobby
> is producing it …
>
> Unbelievably, for the setting for the film a brand-
> new town had been built on an island off the coast of
> Massachusetts. It really looks like you're walking there
> and you're in a different time. It's like a dream.

It was 'amazing' that 'all these plays' by Miller were being produced all at once, said Rebecca. Why was this? 'I really don't know,' her father replied. 'Well, it happens in life, you know. Occasionally, people [producers] suddenly wake up and say, "Oh yeah, that!" and they do them back [restage them]. But I wouldn't take it too seriously. They'll forget about them soon enough.' When Rebecca tells him not to be 'so pessimistic', he responds philosophically with: 'Pessimism is one defence I have against optimism.'[8]

In real life, observed Rebecca, her father was 'prone to walk away from conflict, naturally,' but in his plays, 'there is a continual return of conflict'. To this, Miller replied, 'I suppose it's because there I can live it out, in the literature, in the writing, whereas in life, it was too painful. So, the pain went into the writing, whereas it was hard to sustain it in real life.' Why was that? 'I don't know. I just don't know. I just couldn't bear the idea of people trying to destroy each other, because I sensed early on that all real arguments are murderous. There was a killing instinct in there that I feared, so I put it into theatre.'[9] In other words, for Miller, playwriting was a means of addressing situations which, in reality, he would find unbearable. Furthermore, this act would surely have been a catharsis for him.

Elaborating on the subject further, Miller stated that in his plays, members of his audiences 'need to feel a development, and a rising line of conflict, and a resolution to this, which you can't find in life or rarely find in life. So, the play really gives a resolution, to what

150

doesn't exist in reality.'[10] In any meaningful drama, there has to be conflict, and one gains the impression that as often as not, Miller was agonizing about conflicts in his own life or in the lives of others, conflicts which in real life could not be resolved but which, in the make-believe world of the theatre, *could* find a resolution.

Was her father still writing now, in his later years? Rebecca enquired of him. The answer was yes:

'Writing every day, right up in that building.' 'Plays?' 'Yeah, I'm writing a play now, right up in that building.' This was a reference to a cabin/writing studio in the grounds of his home, which had replaced the original smaller one. 'Don't ask me why, but I love doing it,' he said.

> If you quit, it's one thing. If you're going to go on writing the art is, turn your back on what had worked and go forward to what you think might well work. A human being is many faceted. There are all kinds of different emotions and attitudes that we are all capable of. And you've got to find those that communicate something. The voice is the important thing. That you don't go silent.[11]

Clearly, Miller still felt that he had something important to say, and the joy of writing remained very much alive within him.

Finally, asked Rebecca, what was 'the theme' that was 'pushing' her father to write? 'I think it's less a theme, than an air of wonder and amusement at people and how wonderful they are.' 'It's fun, isn't it?' He laughed uproariously. 'It's all one improvisation after another.'[12]

Chapter 31

Epilogue

Many artists experience lives of excoriating pain, suffering, sorrow, cruelty and injustice, or witness this in others, but few were able to articulate as powerfully the profound emotions that he or she felt as a result of these experiences as Arthur Miller. People express grief, or hurt, or outrage in different ways. Miller, a deeply sensitive person, expressed these sentiments through his plays, and in this way, he was able to share these self-same emotions with an audience that reached far beyond the borders of the USA.

Miller had a unique gift of being able to put himself in the position of others, and feel their pain, albeit vicariously. With his keen intelligence, combined with sensitivity, he was able to get to the heart of what it is to be a human being; and with his wonderful, dry sense of humour, he is able to make us laugh with him and cry with him at the same time. Miller's genius was in creating spoken dialogue and using it with consummate skill to drive his message home. With Miller the playwright, seldom has the expression 'The Pen is Mightier than the Sword' (penned in 1839 by British writer and politician, Edward Bulwer-Lytton) been borne out to such a degree. Many of Miller's essays and plays were based on his own personal experiences. Others were based on other information that came to his attention.

During his lifetime, Miller had many first-hand experiences which became deeply imprinted into his memory, including the ruination of his family in the Wall Street Crash of 1929 and subsequent Great Depression; his infamous persecution by the HUAC; and a traumatic marriage to Marilyn Monroe. He also experienced anti-Semitism at first hand. Miller also learned of the deaths of millions of his Jewish kinsmen and women in the Nazi Holocaust. All of these experiences and many others, were reflected in his plays in which he rails against poverty, injustice, intolerance, racism, human cruelty, unkindness, insincerity, indifference, the futility of war, and the vulnerability and helplessness of human beings when faced with forces beyond their control.

Miller always insisted that the 'common man' was just as susceptible to suffering as everybody else, and he ignored the fact that it was considered to be unfashionable to dwell upon such themes. Yet, he was not alone, for other artistic geniuses like himself were working on similar lines.

Miller was able to express, perhaps like no other, man's vulnerability when faced with forces beyond his control and which threaten to sweep him away. But this is only half of the story because Miller's plays are also about human courage, kindness and self-sacrifice. Miller shows us a way forward, a better way, how we can revise our whole manner of thinking, instead of obsessing with power, possessions, and self-promotion.

Miller's greatness has to do with the fact that his message is universal, and not simply parochial. Said US theatre director and actor, John Tillinger: 'There is a universality to what he's writing, and it's not limited by America. And it is that which makes his plays sing when they're done right.'[1]

Unlike many great thinkers, philosophers, and theologians who, in their lofty arrogance purported to have all the answers, Miller, as far as man's plight is concerned, had the humility to say, no, I do not have all the answers, but at least I can make people conscious of the way they react to adversity, so that in future they may choose a different and better, more productive, and more fulfilling path.

Miller teaches us about endurance, as he perseveres with writing his plays, even in the hardest of times; when he refuses to be intimidated by the power of the HUAC and an overweening state;

when he struggles might and main to help and comfort his wife Marilyn, in her distress.

A study of Arthur Miller's *Collected Essays* reveals the extraordinary breadth of his reading. For he was familiar with the works of numerous literati, dating back to the time of the ancient Greeks. They included playwrights Aeschylus; Bertolt Brecht; Tennessee Williams; Anton Chekhov; Enid Bagnold; Henrik Ibsen; Georg Kaiser; Eugene O'Neill; John Osborne; Jean Giradoux; Thornton Wilder; and Harold Pinter. Also, the philosophers Aristotle and Albert Camus; writers, Samuel Beckett; Fyodor Dostoyevsky; Mark Twain; Marion Starkey; Kenneth Kesey; Thomas Mann; Graham Greene; Leo Tolstoy. Also, philosopher and playwright John-Paul Sartre; playwright and poet, T.S. Eliot; writer and philosopher, Aleksandr Solzhenitsyn; and last, but not least, William Shakespeare.[2]

Those who know Arthur Miller only from film and soundtrack taken in his younger days, may be beguiled into thinking him dour and lacking in humour. And yet, endearingly, he was a home-loving family man, who shunned the limelight and was never happier than when he was in the bosom of his family. It is a joy to see film of him at home in Connecticut with his wife Inge and his family, looking relaxed, smiling, watching her riding her horse, romping with his children, singing even, having achieved worldwide success and recognition, albeit belatedly, in his own country the USA! He was seldom idle, for this was a man who enjoyed making things out of wood, planting trees, collecting logs, driving his tractor; and wherever he went, his two German shepherd dogs followed obediently. As for Inge, she was equally industrious in the home, on the land, and with her photography.

What would Miller wish his obituary to state? 'Writer', he replied modestly. 'That's all. That should say it.'[3]

Miller's brother Kermit died on 17 October 2003 (Arthur's birthday) in Southbury, New Haven, Connecticut, aged 91 years.

He had been married to Frances for fifty-nine years. Frances herself died on 19 June 2004, aged 86.

Arthur Miller died on 10 February 2005 at his home at Roxbury, Connecticut at the age of 89. His first wife, Mary, died on 12 December 2008 at Seaside Terrace, Laguna Beach, California.

Today, at the University of Michigan, and of course elsewhere throughout the world, Miller's plays are performed on a regular basis. The venue is the Arthur Miller Theater, a performing arts theatre in Ann Arbor, Michigan, named in his memory. This came about through the gift of 10 million dollars by Charles Walgreen, who graduated from the university's College of Pharmacy in 1938, for the creation of the Walgreen Drama Center, which would include the theatre. The Arthur Miller Theater was opened on 29 March 2007.

Unlike many, Miller was not content to be an armchair philosopher. For him, life had to be 'hands on', as he battled for freedom of speech; social justice; and social reform; against the waging of war; and especially against corrupt politicians whose sole object was the acquisition of ever more wealth and power for themselves. This quiet, mild-mannered man, had, in fact, a core of steel. He was a doughty warrior who strove might and main to illuminate a path to a better world for everybody: he was the real-life incarnation of John Bunyan's 'Mr Valiant for Truth'. We therefore salute you, Arthur Miller. Thank you, for showing us what our true value should be. In short, for teaching us about love.

Appendix 1

Arthur Miller: Some Awards and Recognitions

1936 (First) Avery Hopwood Award for *No Villain*.

1937 (Second) Avery Hopwood Award for *Honors at Dawn*.

1938 Theatre Guild National award for *They Too Arise* (a revision of *No Villain*).

1947 (First) Tony Award for *All My Sons*.

1949 New York Drama Critics Circle Award for *Death of a Salesman*.

1949 Pulitzer Prize for *Death of a Salesman*.

1949 (Second) Tony Award for *Death of a Salesman*.

1953 (Third) Tony Award for *The Crucible*.

1965 Elected president of International PEN, a worldwide association, founded in London in 1921, to promote literature and intellectual cooperation among writers everywhere.

1970 Creative Arts Award Medal from Brandeis University, Waltham, Massachusetts.

1971 Elected to the American Academy of Arts and Letters.

1973 Appointed adjunct professor in residence at the University of Michigan for the academic year 1973–1974.

1984 Miller and his wife Inge are awarded honorary doctorates from the University of Hartford, West Hartford, Connecticut.

1999 Awarded the Dorothy and Lilian Gish Prize given annually to 'a man or woman who has made an outstanding contribution to the beauty of the world and to mankind's enjoyment and understanding of life'.

Appendix 2

Miller as an Activist

1943 *They May Win* a one-act play in support of the war effort.

1945 Attacks US poet and critic Esra Pound for his pro-fascist activities.

1947 Places an advertisement in the *Daily Worker* protesting about the treatment of German anti-fascist refugees.

1947 Auctions the manuscript of *All My Sons* in aid of the Progressive Citizens of America. This was a left-liberal US political organisation founded in December 1946.

Left liberalism: A variety of liberalism that advocates a regulated market economy and the expansion of civil and political rights.

Liberal favouring individual liberty, free trade, and moderate political and social reform.[1]

1947 Sponsors the World Youth Festival.

1947 His essay 'Subsidized Theater' is published in the *New York Times*.

1964 Appointed special commentator by the *New York Herald Tribune* at the Nazi trials in Frankfurt. Between 1963 and 1976, four trials of members of the Auschwitz concentration camp garrison took place in the German city of Frankfurt.

1968   Attends the Democratic National Convention in Chicago as Eugene McCarthy delegate. McCarthy was a US Democratic politician and poet from Minnesota.

1968   He petitions the Soviet government to lift the ban on the works of Russian writer and political prisoner, Aleksandr Solzhenitsyn.

1969   Refuses to allow his work to be published in Greece in protest of the Greek government's suppression of writers.

1969   *The Reason Why* is a one-act, anti-war allegory. 'Ostensibly about the killing of a woodchuck [groundhog], it was offered as a comment on violence and by implication on Vietnam.'[2] *The Reason Why* was filmed at Miller's home in Connecticut.

1970   He supports a teacher at Roxbury High School who refuses to say the Pledge of Allegiance in the classroom. This was an expression of allegiance to the flag of the USA and to the republic of the USA.

1971   The Brazilian playwright, Augusto Boal is freed from prison with Millers assistance and visits the USA.

1972   Attacked the three-year sentence imposed on US author and publisher, Ralph Ginzberg convinced for obscenity in 1963, the conviction being upheld by the US Supreme Court.

1972   Protests the barring of four Cuban film directors from the USA.

1972   Protests the dismissal of dancer and choreographer, Valery Panov from the Russian Kirov State Dance Theatre for requesting to emigrate.

1974   Urges the United Nations to proclaim that year as 'World Amnesty Year'.

1975 Opposes the actions and resolutions of UNESCO that seek to isolate Israel.

1975 Protest with other literary figures the imprisonment of torture of writers in Iran under the Shah.

1975 Appears before the Senate Permanent Subcommittee on Investigations to support the freedom of writers throughout the world.

1975 Campaigns for a new trial for Peter Reilly, convicted of murdering his mother in Canaan, Connecticut in September 1973.

1977 Joins other literary figures in signing a letter to the Czech head of state, Gustav Husak protesting the arrest of dissidents.

1978 Joins the protest march and rally to the Soviet Mission to the United Nations, New York City, protesting the arrest of dissidents including the Russian journalist, poet, human rights activist, dissident, and political prisoner, Alexander Ginzburg (1936-2002), and Soviet-Israeli dissident, human rights advocate, and political prisoner, Anatoly Shcharansky (b. 1948).

1979 Joins march to the Czech United Nations Mission in New York City protesting the violation of the 1975 Helsinki Accords. This was an agreement signed by thirty-five nations on 1 August 1975 that concluded the Conference on Security and Cooperation in Europe.

1980 Joins other US Jews in signing letter with other American Jews protesting the expansion of Jewish settlements on Israel's West Bank under the government of Israel's prime minister Menachem Begin.

1980 Joins other writers in signing a letter in support of the Polish Solidarity Movement, founded on 14 August 1980 by shipyard electrician, Lech Walesa in the Lenin (now Gdańsk) shipyards. This was Poland's first independent trade union movement, and it gave rise to an anti-communist movement which contributed greatly to the fall of communism in Europe.

1982   Attempts, unsuccessfully, to save two Broadway theatres from demolition.

1982   Joins other playwrights in opposing a lawsuit brought by Broadway producers to limit the earnings of dramatists.

1985   Contributes 50,000 dollars to the Hopwood Visiting Writers Fund at the University of Michigan.

1985   Travels with British playwright Harold Pinter to Istanbul in support of Turkish writers.

1985   Protests an immigration law that denies permanent residence to certain artists.[3]

Notes

Chapter 1: The Miller Family: from Austro-Hungary to New York City

1. Miller, Arthur, *Timebends: A Life*, p.8.
2. Bigsby, Christopher, *Arthur Miller 1915–1962*, p.4.
3. Ibid, p.12.
4. Miller, Arthur, op. cit., p.9.
5. Bigsby, Christopher, op. cit., p.13.
6. Ibid, pp.12-13.
7. Ibid, p.19
8. *Arthur Miller: Writer: A Film by Rebecca Miller*, 2018.
9. Ibid.
10. Bigsby, Christopher, op. cit., p.20
11. Ibid, p.13.
12. *Arthur Miller: Writer: A Film by Rebecca Miller*, 2018.
13. Ibid.
14. 'Arthur Miller', The South Bank Show, 2019.

Chapter 2: Childhood and Youth

1. 'Arthur Miller', The South Bank Show, 2019.
2. *Arthur Miller: Writer: A Film by Rebecca Miller*, 2018.
3. Ibid.
4. Schlueter, June, and James K. Flanigan, *Arthur Miller*, p.ix.
5. *Arthur Miller: Writer: A Film by Rebecca Miller*, 2018.

Chapter 3: The University of Michigan (1934 to 1938): Early Success: Miller the Idealist

1. *Wikipedia.*
2. Herman, Judi, 'Review: *No Villain*: The World Premiere of a Vital Addition to Arthur Miller's Canon of Work – His Very First Play', *Jewish Renaissance*, Reviews, Theatre, 27 June 2016.
3. 'Arthur Miller', Interview and Clips, 2001', YouTube, 25 June 2008.
4. *Arthur Miller: Writer: A Film by Rebecca Miller*, 2018.
5. Bigsby, Christopher, *Arthur Miller 1915–1962*, p.135.
6. Miller, Arthur, *Timebends: A Life*, p.105.
7. Stevenson, A., and Waite, M., *Concise Oxford English Dictionary*.
8. Miller, Arthur, op. cit., p.111.

Chapter 4: The Second World War (1 September 1939 to 2 September 1945): Marriage (1st) to Mary Grace Slattery (5 August 1940).

1. *Arthur Miller: Writer: A Film by Rebecca Miller*, 2018.
2. Ibid.
3. Ibid.
4. Arthur Miller: 'Conversation at the University of Michigan', YouTube, 2001.
5. Abbotson, Susan C. W., *Arthur Miller: A Literary Reference*, p.431.

Chapter 5: *The Man Who Had All the Luck* (1944): *All My Sons* (1947): *The Hook* (1947)

1. *Arthur Miller: Writer: A Film by Rebecca Miller*, 2018.
2. 'Arthur Miller', The South Bank Show, 2019.

3. *Arthur Miller: Writer: A Film by Rebecca Miller*, 2018.
4. 'Arthur Miller', interviewed by Charlie Rose, YouTube, 3 July 1992.
5. *Arthur Miller: Writer: A Film by Rebecca Miller*, 2018.
6. 'Arthur Miller', Interview and Clips, 2001', YouTube, 25 June 2008
7. *Arthur Miller: Writer: A Film by Rebecca Miller*, 2018.
8. 'Arthur Miller', interviewed by Charlie Rose, YouTube, 3 July 1992.

Chapter 6: Married Life: Miller as a Father: Miller in Psychoanalysis

1. *Arthur Miller: Writer: A Film by Rebecca Miller*, 2018.
2. Ibid.
3. Arthur Miller: 'Interview on his Life and Career' by Mike Wallace, YouTube, 1987.
4. Miller, Arthur, *Timebends: A Life*, p.320.
5. Arthur Miller: 'The Meaning of Suffering', Youtube, 1963,

Chapter 7: Ezra Pound and Ernie Pyle

1. Stevenson, A., and Waite, M., *Concise Oxford English Dictionary*.
2. Miller, Arthur, 'Should Ezra Pound be Shot? Five Writers Indict Him as a Traitor', *New Masses*, 25 December 1945.
3. Miller, Arthur, 'Ernie Pyle: GI', *New Masses*, 15 May 1945.

Chapter 8: *Death of a Salesman* (1949)

1. 'Arthur Miller', interviewed by Charlie Rose, YouTube, 3 July 1992.
2. 'Arthur Miller', The South Bank Show, 2019.

3. *Arthur Miller: Writer: A Film by Rebecca Miller*, 2018.
4. Ibid.
5. Miller, Arthur, *Timebends: A Life*, pp.183-4.
6. 'Arthur Miller', Interview and Clips, 2001', YouTube, 25 June 2008.
7. *Arthur Miller: Writer: A Film by Rebecca Miller*, 2018.
8. 'Arthur Miller', interviewed by Charlie Rose, YouTube, 3 July 1992.
9. *Arthur Miller: Writer: A Film by Rebecca Miller*, 2018.
10. Ibid.

Chapter 9: Miller's Uncle Emmanuel ('Manny') Newman

1. *Arthur Miller: Writer: A Film by Rebecca Miller*, 2018.
2. Lahr, John H., 'Walking with Arthur Miller', 1999, *The New Yorker*, 1 March 2012.
3. Emmanuel Newman, Certificate of Death, Certificate Number 8767, Bureau for Records, Department of Health, Kings, Brooklyn.

Chapter 10: The Waldorf Conference (25-27 March 1949)

1. Klefstad, Terry, 'Shostakovich and the Peace Conference', *Music & Politics*, Volume 6, Issue 2, Summer 2012.
2. 'Arthur Miller Interview', Parts 1:1-1.3, YouTube, 22 September 2008.
3. Miller, Arthur, *Timebends*, p.237.
4. Ibid, p.236.
5. Ibid, p.239.

Chapter 11: *The Crucible* (1953)

1. Soanes, Catherine and Angus Stevenson (editors), *Oxford Dictionary of English*.
2. *Arthur Miller: Writer: A Film by Rebecca Miller*, 2018.
3. Arthur Miller, interview, Parts 1:1-3, YouTube, 22-23 September 2008.
4. *Arthur Miller: Writer: A Film by Rebecca Miller*, 2018.
5. Stevenson, A., and Waite, M., *Concise Oxford English Dictionary*.
6. 'Arthur Miller Interview', Parts 1:1-1.3, YouTube, 22 September 2008.
7. 'Arthur Miller', interviewed by Charlie Rose, YouTube, 3 July 1992.
8. 'Arthur Miller Interview', Parts 1:1-1.3, YouTube, 22 September 2008.
9. Ibid.
10. Ibid.
11. Stevenson, A., and Waite, M., op. cit.
12. Soanes, Catherine and Angus Stevenson (editors), op. cit.
13. *Wikipedia*.
14. Soanes, Catherine and Angus Stevenson (editors), op. cit.
15. CULTURE, HISTORY, HISTORY & CULTURE: 'The (A) History Of Witches', posted by CASSI, 8 October 2019.
16. Soanes, Catherine and Angus Stevenson (editors), op. cit.
17. Kushiym, Sayfullah ibn Yehud al-Isuni ibn, 'Witchcraft: Mistranslation of Bible Revisionists and Dates of Revision', Academia.edu online.
18. 'Arthur Miller Interview', Parts 1:1-1.3, YouTube, 22 September 2008.
19. Ibid.
20. Flood, Alison, 'Arthur Miller Scorned Public Mourners of Marilyn Monroe, Archive Sale Reveals', *The Guardian*, 11 January 2018.

Chapter 12: The House Un-American Activities Committee (HUAC)

1. 'Communist Control Act of 1954', *Wikipedia*.
2. Bigsby, Christopher, *Arthur Miller 1915–1962*, p.290.
3. *Arthur Miller: Writer: A Film by Rebecca Miller*, 2018.
4. 'Arthur Miller', interviewed by Charlie Rose, YouTube, 3 July 1992.
5. 'Martin Gottfried on Elia Kazan: Arthur Miller and Naming Names', Theatertalk, YouTube, 10 March 2014.
6. Arthur Miller: 'Interview on his Life and Career' by Mike Wallace, YouTube, 1987.
7. 'Arthur Miller', interviewed by Charlie Rose, YouTube, 3 July 1992.
8. Arthur Miller: 'Interview on his Life and Career' by Mike Wallace, YouTube, 1987.

Chapter 13: *A View from the Bridge* (1955)

1. '*A View from the Bridge*', Parts 1.1 to 1.5, YouTube, 24 February 2013.

Chapter 14: Marriage (2nd) to Marilyn Monroe (29 June 1956): The Vietnam War

1. *Arthur Miller: Writer: A Film by Rebecca Miller*, 2018.
2. Arthur Miller, Interview, YouTube, 1987.
3. Ibid.
4. 'Arthur Miller', interviewed by Charlie Rose, YouTube, 3 July 1992.

5. 'Treated Me as a Sensitive Person: Marilyn Monroe on Arthur Miller', YouTube, 31 December 2015.
6. *Arthur Miller: Writer: A Film by Rebecca Miller*, 2018.
7. Dowd, Maureen, 'Rebecca Miller on the Mother of All Subjects: Her Father', *New York Times*, 11 March 2008.
8. *Arthur Miller: Writer: A Film by Rebecca Miller*, 2018.
9. Arthur Miller: 'Interview on his Life and Career' by Mike Wallace, YouTube, 1987.
10. *Arthur Miller: Writer: A Film by Rebecca Miller*, 2018.

Chapter 15: Miller's Testimony to the HUAC (21 June 1956)

1. Investigation of the Unauthorized Use of US Passports: Hearing: Before the Committee on Un-American Activities, House of Representatives, Eighty-fourth Congress, Second Session, p.1353.
2. *Wikipedia*
3. Arthur Miller: 'Interview on his Life and Career' by Mike Wallace, YouTube, 1987.
4. Investigation of the Unauthorized Use of US Passports: Hearing: Before the Committee on Un-American Activities, House of Representatives, Eighty-fourth Congress, Second Session, pp.4656-4691.
5. Thacker, David, 'Arthur Miller on Trial', *Independent*, 1 March 2006.
6. 'Arthur Miller Interview', Parts 1:1-1.3, YouTube, 22 September 2008.
7. *Arthur Miller: Writer: A Film by Rebecca Miller*, 2018.
8. 'Playwright Arthur Miller on Communism, 1971', CBC Archives, CBC-YouTube, 2 February 2011.
9. Abbotson, Susan C. W., *Arthur Miller: A Literary Reference*, p.11.

10. 'Executive Sessions of the Senate Permanent Subcommittee on Investigations of the Committee on Government Operations', Volume 1, Eighty-Third Congress, First Session, 1953. *US Government Printing Office*, 2003. Preface.

Chapter 16: John Steinbeck: a Staunch Ally

1. Steinbeck, John, 'The Trial of Arthur Miller', *Esquire*, 1 June 1957.
2. Chilton, Martin, 'John Steinbeck: A Flawed Genius', *Independent*, 20 December 2018.
3. 'Arthur Miller Receives the 1999 Steinbeck Award': The Martha Heasley Cox Center for Steinbeck Studies, San José State University, San José, California.
4. Ibid.

Chapter 17: *The Misfits* (1961)

1. 'Arthur Miller: *The Misfits*: American Values', YouTube, 15 February 2012.
2. *Arthur Miller: Writer: A Film by Rebecca Miller*, 2018.
3. 'Arthur Miller: *The Misfits*: American Values', YouTube, 15 February 2012.
4. *Arthur Miller: Writer: A Film by Rebecca Miller*, 2018.
5. Ibid.
6. 'Arthur Miller', interviewed by Charlie Rose, YouTube, 3 July 1992.
7. Arthur Miller, Interview, YouTube, 1987.
8. 'Arthur Miller', interviewed by Charlie Rose, YouTube, 3 July 1992.
9. Arthur Miller, Interview, YouTube, 1987.
10. *Arthur Miller: Writer: A Film by Rebecca Miller*, 2018.

Chapter 18: Miller and Marilyn's Marriage: the Clouds Gather: Divorce

1. Arthur Miller, Interview, YouTube, 1987.
2. 'Arthur Miller', interviewed by Charlie Rose, YouTube, 3 July 1992.
3. Ibid.
4. Miller, Arthur, *Timebends: A Life*, p.468.
5. 'Arthur Miller', interviewed by Charlie Rose, YouTube, 3 July 1992.
6. Ibid.
7. *Arthur Miller: Writer: A Film by Rebecca Miller*, 2018.
8. Miller, Arthur, op. cit., pp.415,483.
9. Arthur Miller: 'Interview on his Life and Career' by Mike Wallace, YouTube, 1987.
10. Arthur Miller, Interview, YouTube, 1987.
11. Ibid.
12. *Arthur Miller: Writer: A Film by Rebecca Miller*, 2018.
13. Ibid.
14. *Arthur Miller: Writer: A Film by Rebecca Miller*, 2018.
15. 'Arthur Miller', interviewed by Charlie Rose, YouTube, 3 July 1992.
16. *Arthur Miller: Writer: A Film by Rebecca Miller*, 2018.

Chapter 19: The Death of Marilyn and its Effect on Miller: Ingeborg Morath

1. 'Arthur Miller', interviewed by Charlie Rose, YouTube, 3 July 1992.
2. Miller, Arthur, *Timebends: A Life*, p.531.
3. This essay was part of the extensive archive of manuscripts, notebooks, and letters, donated by Miller to the Harry Ransom Center, University of Texas at Austin in 1961/1962.

4. Flood, Alison, 'Arthur Miller Scorned Public Mourners of Marilyn Monroe, Archive Sale Reveals', *The Guardian*, 11 January 2018.
5. Norman, Andrew, *Making Sense of Marilyn*, p.135.
6. First, M.B. and N. Ward, (editorial and coding consultants), *Diagnostic and Statistical Manual of Mental Disorders, Fifth Edition, DSM-5™*, p.663.
7. Arthur Miller, Interview, YouTube, 1987.
8. *Arthur Miller: Writer: A Film by Rebecca Miller*, 2018.
9. Ibid.

Chapter 20: *After the Fall* (1964): *Incident at Vichy* (1964): *The Price* (1968): *The Creation of the World and Other Business* (1972)

1. Arthur Miller, Interview, YouTube, 1987.
2. Soanes, Catherine and Angus Stevenson (editors), op. cit.
3. Arthur Miller, Interview, YouTube, 1987.
4. Ibid.
5. *Arthur Miller: Writer: A Film by Rebecca Miller*, 2018.
6. 'Arthur Miller', interviewed by Charlie Rose, YouTube, 3 July 1992.
7. Bigsby, Christopher, *Arthur Miller 1915–1962*, p.399.
8. 'Arthur Miller', interviewed by Charlie Rose, YouTube, 3 July 1992.
9. *Arthur Miller: Writer: A Film by Rebecca Miller*, 2018.
10. Ibid.

Chapter 21: Miller at Home: Humour; Gaiety; Contentment

1. *Arthur Miller: Writer: A Film by Rebecca Miller*, 2018.
2. Ibid.
3. Ibid.

4. *The Atheism Tapes with Jonathan Miller*: Arthur Miller, BBC, 2003.
5. *Arthur Miller: Writer: A Film by Rebecca Miller*, 2018.
6. Ibid.
7. Ibid.
8. Ibid.

Chapter 22: Daniel Miller

1. Stevenson, A., and Waite, M., *Concise Oxford English Dictionary*.
2. *Arthur Miller: Writer: A Film by Rebecca Miller*, 2018.
3. Andrews, Suzanne, 'Arthur Miller's Missing Act', *Vogue Business*, 13 September 2007.
4. NADS: National Association for Down Syndrome, 'History of NADS', online.

Chapter 23: Miller's Disillusionment with Marxism/ Communism: Religion and the Afterlife

1. Soanes, Catherine and Angus Stevenson (editors), op. cit.
2. Ibid
3. *Arthur Miller: Writer: A Film by Rebecca Miller*, 2018.
4. Bigsby, Christopher, *Arthur Miller 1915–1962*, p.177.
5. Bigsby, Christopher, interview with Arthur Miller, 2003, Bigsby, Christopher, op. cit., p.358.
6. Bigsby, Christopher, op. cit., p.366.
7. Miller, Arthur, *Timebends: A Life*, p.395.
8. Ibid, pp.407-8.
9. *The Atheism Tapes with Jonathan Miller*: Arthur Miller, BBC, 2003.
10. Ibid.
11. Ibid.

Chapter 24: Anti-Semitism: The Danger of Religion Wedded to Nationalism

1. *The Atheism Tapes with Jonathan Miller*: Arthur Miller, BBC, 2003.
2. Stevenson, A., and Waite, M., *Concise Oxford English Dictionary*.
3. Ibid.
4. *The Atheism Tapes with Jonathan Miller*: Arthur Miller, BBC, 2003.

Chapter 25: Miller: an Abhorrence of Racism

1. Bigsby, Christopher, *Arthur Miller 1915–1962*, pp.180-181.
2. Ibid, p.91
3. Ibid, pp.190-1. Christopher Bigsby, interview with Arthur Miller, October 2003.
4. Roudané, Matthew, *The Collected Essays of Arthur Miller*, p.337.

Chapter 26: 1992: The State of the Theatre

1. 'Arthur Miller', interviewed by Charlie Rose, YouTube, 3 July 1992.
2. Ibid.
3. Ibid.
4. Ibid.

Chapter 27: Miller's Opinion of US Politicians

1. Jones, David R., 'Party Polarisation and Legislative Gridlock', *Political Research Quarterly*, Volume 54, Number 1, March 2001, pp.125-141.
2. 'Arthur Miller', Charlie Rose, YouTube, 3 July 1992.
3. Stevenson, A., and Waite, M., *Concise Oxford English Dictionary*.

4. 'Arthur Miller', Charlie Rose, YouTube, 3 July 1992.
5. Stevenson, A., and Waite, M., op. cit.

Chapter 28: Some Other Plays and Writings: *Mr Peters' Connections* (1998)

1. Arthur Miller: 'Conversation at the University of Michigan', YouTube, 2001.
2. Martin, Robert A., and Steven R Centola, *The Theater Essays of Arthur Miller*, p.193.
3. Bigsby, Christopher, *Arthur Miller 1915–1962*, p.27.
4. 'Arthur Miller', interviewed by Charlie Rose, YouTube, 3 July 1992.
5. Stevenson, A., and Waite
6. *Arthur Miller: Writer: A Film by Rebecca Miller*, 2018.
7. Miller, Arthur, *Mr Peters' Connections*, Preface.
8. *Arthur Miller: Writer: A Film by Rebecca Miller*, 2018.

Chapter 29: *Finishing the Picture* (2004): Later Years

1. Norman, Andrew, *Making Sense of Marilyn*, p.101.
2. Miller, Arthur, *Timebends: A Life*, p.599.
3. *Arthur Miller: Writer: A Film by Rebecca Miller*, 2018.

Chapter 30: Arthur Miller the Playwright

1. 'Arthur Miller', interviewed by Charlie Rose, YouTube, 3 July 1992.
2. *Arthur Miller: Writer: A Film by Rebecca Miller*, 2018.
3. 'Arthur Miller', interviewed by Charlie Rose, YouTube, 3 July 1992.

4. *Arthur Miller: Writer: A Film by Rebecca Miller*, 2018.
5. 'Arthur Miller', The South Bank Show, 2019.
6. Ibid.
7. Ibid.
8. *Arthur Miller: Writer: A Film by Rebecca Miller*, 2018.
9. Ibid.
10. 'Arthur Miller', interviewed by Charlie Rose, YouTube, 3 July 1992.
11. *Arthur Miller: Writer: A Film by Rebecca Miller*, 2018.
12. Ibid.

Chapter 31: Epilogue

1. Arthur Miller at 100, Westport County Playhouse, 2015.
2. Roudané, Matthew, *The Collected Essays of Arthur Miller*.v
3. *Arthur Miller: Writer: A Film by Rebecca Miller*, 2018.

Appendix 2: Miller as an Activist

1. Stevenson, A., and Waite, M., *Concise Oxford English Dictionary*.
2. Bigsby, Christopher, Arthur Miller 1962-2005, Phoenix, London, 2009.
3. Source: Schlueter, June, and James K. Flanigan, *Arthur Miller*.

Bibliography

Abbotson, Susan C.W., *Arthur Miller: A Literary Reference* (Facts on File, New York, 2007)

Bigsby, Christopher, *Arthur Miller 1915–1962* (Phoenix, London, 2009)

First, M.B. and Ward, N. (editorial and coding consultants), *Diagnostic and Statistical Manual of Mental Disorders, Fifth Edition, DSM-5*™ (Washington D.C., American Psychiatric Publishing, 2013)

Martin, Robert A., and Steven R. Centola, *The Theater Essays of Arthur Miller* (New York, 1996)

Miller, Arthur, *Timebends: A Life* (Grove Press, New York, 1987)

Norman, Andrew, *Making Sense of Marilyn* (Fonthill, Stroud, UK, 2018)

Roudané, Matthew, *The Collected Essays of Arthur Miller* (Bloomsbury, London, and New York, 2015)

Schlueter, June, and James K. Flanigan, *Arthur Miller* (Ungar, New York, 1987)

Stevenson, A., and Waite, M., *Concise Oxford English Dictionary*, (Oxford and New York, Oxford University Press, 2011)

'Sutcliffe, Jessica, *Face: Shape and Angle: Helen Muspratt Photographer* (Manchester University Press, UK, 2016)

Documentary Film

The Atheism Tapes with Jonathan Miller: 'Arthur Miller'.

'Arthur Miller, Interview and Clips, 2001', YouTube, 25 June 2008.

Arthur Miller: 'Conversation at the University of Michigan', YouTube, 2001.

'Arthur Miller': interviewed by Charlie Rose, YouTube, 3 July 1992.

Arthur Miller: 'Interview on his Life and Career' by Mike Wallace, YouTube, 1987.

Arthur Miller: 'The Meaning of Suffering', 1963, Youtube.

'Arthur Miller Interview', Parts 1:1-1.3, YouTube, 22 September 2008.

'Martin Gottfried on Elia Kazan: Arthur Miller and Naming Names', Theatertalk, YouTube, 10 March 2014.

'Playwright Arthur Miller on Communism, 1971', CBC Archives, CBC-YouTube, 2 February 2011.

'*A View from the Bridge*', Parts 1.1 to 1.5, YouTube, 24 February 2013.

'Charlie Chaplin', BBC interview, YouTube, 1954.

'Joan Baez on Activism, Vietnam, and the Guitar', YouTube.

'Treated Me as a Sensitive Person: Marilyn Monroe on Arthur Miller', YouTube, 31 December 2015.

Arthur Miller: Writer: A Film by Rebecca Miller. A Round Films Production (for HBO Documentary Films, Keystrike Pictures, Inc., released 8 December 2017)

'Arthur Miller: *The Misfits*: American Values', YouTube, 15 February 2012.

Arthur Miller, Interview, YouTube, 1987.

Classic Clips, 'Arthur Miller: Playwright: Working in the Theatre', YouTube, 1986.

'Arthur Miller', The South Bank Show, broadcast 9 November 1980, edited and presented by Melvin Bragg, Sky UK Ltd, 2019.

By the Same Author

By Swords Divided: Corfe Castle in the Civil War. Halsgrove, 2003.

Thomas Hardy: Christmas Carollings. Halsgrove, 2005.

Enid Blyton and her Enchantment with Dorset. Halsgrove, 2005.

Tyneham: A Tribute. Halsgrove, 2007.

Agatha Christie: The Finished Portrait. Tempus, 2007.

The Story of George Loveless and the Tolpuddle Martyrs. Halsgrove, 2008.

Father of the Blind: A Portrait of Sir Arthur Pearson. The History Press, 2009.

Agatha Christie: The Pitkin Guide. Pitkin Publishing, 2009.

Arthur Conan Doyle: The Man behind Sherlock Holmes. The History Press, 2009.

HMS Hood: Pride of the Royal Navy. The History Press, 2009.

Purbeck Personalities. Halsgrove, 2009.

Bournemouth's Founders and Famous Visitors. The History Press, 2010.

Thomas Hardy: Behind the Mask. The History Press, 2011.

A Brummie Boy goes to War. Halsgrove, 2011.

Winston Churchill: Portrait of an Unquiet Mind. Pen & Sword Books, 2012.

Charles Darwin: Destroyer of Myths. Pen & Sword Books, 2013.

Beatrix Potter: Her Inner World. Pen & Sword Books, 2013.

T.E. Lawrence: Tormented Hero. Fonthill, 2014.

Agatha Christie: The Disappearing Novelist. Fonthill, 2014.

Lawrence of Arabia's Clouds Hill. Halsgrove, 2014.

Jane Austen: Love is Like a Rose. Fonthill, 2015.

Kindly Light: The Story of Blind Veterans UK. Fonthill, 2015.

Thomas Hardy at Max Gate: The Latter Years. Halsgrove, 2016.

Corfe Remembered. Halsgrove, 2017.

Thomas Hardy: Bockhampton and Beyond. Halsgrove, 2017.

Mugabe: Monarch of Blood and Tears. Austin Macauley, 2017

Making Sense of Marilyn. Fonthill, 2018.

Hitler's Insanity: A Conspiracy of Silence. Fonthill, 2018.

The Unwitting Fundamentalist. Austin Macauley, 2018.

Robert Mugabe's Lost Jewel of Africa. Fonthill, 2018.

Hitler: Dictator or Puppet? Pen & Sword, 2011, 2020.

Halsewell: A Shipwreck that Gripped the Nation. Fonthill, 2020.

Author's website https://www.andrew-norman.co.uk

Index

Index

Index